Faith A. Oyedepo

Building A Successful Family

Contents

Introduction

Topmost on the counselling list of churches and counselling centres are family related issues. So many people have questions on the family, for which very few seem to have adequate answers. Yet, a great family or household is part of a man's testimony. Whatever success a man or woman will enjoy in any area of life, begins with a great family or household.

God, the designer of marriage and the family, recounting the virtues of Job, did not only make mention of his character traits and assets, but also specifically mentioned his family.

There was a man in the land of Uz, whose name was Job; and that man was perfect and upright, and one that feared God, and eschewed evil.

And there were born unto him seven sons and three daughters.

His substance also was seven thousand sheep, and three thousand camels, and five hundred yoke of oxen, and five hundred she asses, and a very great household; so that this man was the greatest of all the men of the east.

Job 1:1-3 (Emphasis mine)

From this account, it is quite obvious that a man's testimony is not complete without a mention of the state of his family. Family success is the foundation for all-round success. Any man who succeeds as the head of his family is sure to succeed in anything else in life. No matter what level of success a man or woman attains in life, if it is not accompanied by an undeniable family success, such success or accomplishment will be unsustainable. Society is replete with several great destinies that have crashed due to the failure in the family setup. Social, financial, business or career success (even with fame and all) without family success is tasteless and frustrating.

God designed the family for success and not failure! He proved this by being practically involved in the institution of the first marriage, and subsequently the family. Take a closer look at this passage:

And the Lord God caused a deep sleep to fall upon Adam, and he slept: and he took one of his ribs, and closed up the flesh instead thereof;

And the rib, which the Lord God had taken from man, made he a woman, and brought her unto the man.

Genesis 2:21-22

When the first marriage was instituted, God did not just speak it into existence like He did the rest of creation. He was practically involved in its institution.

There is no limit to the pleasures and blessings God can bring to all areas of your life, through a successful family life. There is a joy that comes along with family success. This joy simply spills over into every area of life. Joy entreats divine presence, and with divine presence comes *"pleasures for evermore"* (Ps. 16:11).

The family can be likened to a highly valuable product. Just as every product requires necessary raw materials before it can be produced and function excellently, so also the family cannot function successfully until relevant raw materials are fully processed.

Joshua 1:8 shows us the factory from where all the raw materials for family success can be obtained:

> *This book of the law shall not depart out of thy mouth; but thou shalt meditate therein day and night, that thou mayest observe to do according to all that is written therein: for then thou shalt make thy way prosperous, and then thou shalt have good success.*

"This book of the law" or the Word of God is the factory for family success. It is full of principles which, when processed and practiced, are bound to deliver, not just success, but good success. A successful home

is dependent on a total adherence to biblical marriage principles.

Success in all areas of life is God's will for you. But it does not come by chance, neither is it an accidental occurrence. Nothing successful can be classified as an accident, as no accident is a testimony.

I am yet to find a man or woman who succeeded in his/her family by chance, who woke up after 50 years and just discovered that they had made it! It never happens, because success is not a gift! It is neither a product of luck nor chance. It does not just happen. It takes conscious, deliberate, and calculated steps to realise success in any venture, including the family.

The fact that many are frustrated, unhappy, fed up, and failing does not, however, tamper with the truth of God's Word. The family is designed for success! This truth must be appreciated in order for it to be appropriated. That is precisely why the later part of Joshua 1:8 says:

... Then thou shalt have good success.

If you are married and experiencing turbulence in your family, all you need do is to apply the principles contained in God's Word and the storms will cease. If you are about to begin your own family, you can avoid frustration by operating the principles contained in the

Word of God. If, however, your family is one that can be termed "successful," it can move up to the realm of good success! For success to remain success, it must be constantly improved upon. Success today that is not improved upon will become failure tomorrow. The largest room in the world is the room for improvement.

A better tomorrow awaits your family! That is why, I believe, God instructed me to write this book: so that you can enjoy God's best. I believe only the best is good enough for you.

Happy reading!

Understanding The Family

So God created man in his own image, in the image of God created he him; male and female created he them.

And God blessed them, and God said unto them, Be fruitful, and multiply, and replenish the earth...

Genesis 1:27-28

No nation can be better than the health of the individual families that make up that nation, because the nucleus unit of any nation and any people, tribe or race, even the smallest nation, is the family. It stands as a fundamental social group of a typical society.

Mother Theresa, the great saintly woman of God and founder of the Order of the Missionaries of Charity, when asked what the solution to world peace was, said, "Let every one go home and love their families." She was literally saying that the chaos in the world today, has its foundation in the way the family structure and family values are being misunderstood and misused.

The Family Unit

The word "family" in the Longman's Dictionary of Contemporary English means: a group of people who are closely related to each other, especially mother, father, and their children representing the nuclear family. There is also, however, the extended family set up, which include aunts, uncles, grandparents, distant relations, etc.

The family unit can also be defined as two or more people who share common goals and values, have a long-term commitment to one another, a common ancestry, and usually reside in the same dwelling place, under one roof or live in the same house.

Another word for "family" from the Bible is "household" or "house of" as in Psalm 115:12. Speaking about God's desire for the family circle, it says:

> *... He will bless the house of Israel; he will bless the house of Aaron.*

Also, Genesis 18:19 says:

> *For I know him, that he will command his children and his household after him ...*

In this passage we see that "household" refers to more

than just husband, wife, and children, because the word "children" had already been mentioned before the word "household." A household has much more than just husband, wife and children, but can refer to all who live under that roof and authority of the householder or owner of the house. Such persons may include close relations, distant relations, in-laws, servants, housemaids and domestic staff (some people have their drivers, gardeners, security personnel, etc., living with them under the same roof, and treat them as members of their family).

The Marriage Relationship

Marriage is the legal union of a man and a woman as husband and wife. It is the foundation on which the lives and relationship of family members are initiated or built.

The Longman's dictionary defines marriage as a relationship between two people who are married or who have been joined together as husband and wife according to the law, custom, or church demands.

Although, having children is one of the blessings of marriage, marriage means much more than just having children or co-habiting with someone of the opposite sex. Marriage is actually a covenant, a fusion, a blending of a man and a woman in a life long, inseparable relationship. It is an agreement and commitment of two people before witnesses. It is a relational structure through which a man and a woman join as husband and wife, become one flesh, and together rule in earthly dominion.

It is two people, specifically a man and a woman, a husband and a wife, coming together to pledge their lives and commitment to each other, about forming a family or building a household together.

God is the originator of the first marriage. In Genesis 2:18, the Bible says:

> **And the LORD God said, It is not good that the man should be alone; I will make him an help meet for him.**

The subsequent verses show how God went about doing just that. God showed His interest in marriage, by personally fashioning the woman and delivering her to her husband. He was personally present at the first marriage ceremony (Gen. 2: 21-23). What's more? The first miracle ever that Jesus performed during His earthly ministry, was at a marriage ceremony at Cana of Galilee, where He turned water into wine, restoring the missing joy and excitement in that marriage (Jn. 2:1-11).

Does your marriage seem to be joyless right now? Do not lose hope. God who did it at Cana, will do it again in your life, and will give you a miracle, because He is still a miracle worker Expect a miracle! However, you must be ready to obey His instructions, like they did at the wedding in Cana, before their water was turned into wine. Read this testimony carefully.

"I had suffered all manner of cruel oppositions and harassments because I could not conceive. My in-laws had abused me verbally and physically, and put pressure on my husband to kick me out of my matrimonial home. Finally, he succumbed and sent me packing. Because I really had no where to go, I was literally squatting from one concerned neighbour's house to the other, all the while seeking reconciliation.

When I learnt of the oncoming Family Renewal Convention, I determined to serve the Lord, and God did it! He granted me favour before my husband, who called me back to our home, and shortly after the reunion, I discovered I was pregnant. My home was not only restored, I conceived as well. The convention brought double blessings to me."

– Amaka, D.

Double blessings await you as well. Your testimony shall be the next!

God, as the originator of marriage, is the foundation for a successful marriage. Building your home upon

Him, will ensure a successful family life. However, many couples push God and His principles aside, and yet expect to enjoy divine benefits and blessings in their marriage and family life. It cannot work that way, as the place you give God in your life determines your overall placement in life.

Marriage Versus the Family

Fredrick K. C. Price said, "Marriage is a divine ordinance. Without marriage as a divine ordinance you cannot have a family. You may have a group of people living in the same house, but you cannot have a family. You will have a living arrangement, but not godly relationships."

In other words, if there is no marriage, there can be no family, because there is a decent order and process to follow in establishing a family. The Bible admonishes this:

Let all things be done decently and in order.
1 Corinthians 14:40

The marriage relationship, though essential to the family unit, differs from family relationship. Let's see how.

Firstly, marriage is between two parties, man and woman, husband and wife. It is between two people of the **opposite sex** only. It is important to make this point very clear here, especially in these "modern" days of "same sex marriages". Even though same sex marriages may be acceptable to the society, it is not acceptable to God. For: *"... Male and female created he them."* -Genesis 1:27 *"Therefore shall a man ...cleave unto his wife..."* -Genesis 2:24

Notice the words "male", "female", "man", and "wife" in the above scriptures. These all point to two people of the opposite sex, not same sex. God is a God of details. To have God's kind of marriage, things must be done His own way. Following the crowd and doing what everybody else is doing, can never make for success in marriage. Caution! Caution!! Caution!!! God warns in His word:

> *...Be not deceived: neither fornicators, nor idolaters, nor adulterers, nor effeminate (homosexuals), nor abusers of themselves with mankind ... shall inherit the kingdom of God.*
>
> 1 Corinthians 6:9-10

To go against the word of God is for life to go against you! The scriptures cannot be broken. To attempt to break scriptures, is to be broken in life. Those who make light of God's word, are naturally victims in life.

The family on the other hand, involves at least two, and eventually more people.

Secondly, marriage is a covenant, resulting in a fusion, a blending and a life long relationship between one man and one woman. The husband and wife relationship is established by covenant.

Marriage is not just a good idea; it is God's idea. God instituted it; it is divine. It is not a **cultural** thing, but a **scriptural** thing. It is not a product of man's arrangement, but God's arrangement.

A family tie, however, is a common ancestral or associational bond resulting in a connecting cord between the individuals within that same family. Its existence is not necessarily by their own volition. That is, you really have no say in deciding which family to belong to.

> **And Judah said unto his brethren ... he is our brother and our flesh...**
>
> Genesis 37:26-27

Thirdly, marriage is by choice; each party chooses to become bonded. In a family, however, each member is bonded as a result of their common ancestry, whether or not they choose to. In Genesis 28:2, Isaac told Jacob his son:

> **Arise, go to Padan-aram, to the house of Bethuel thy mother's father; and take thee a wife from thence of the daughters of Laban thy mother's brother.**

The marriage relationship in which you find yourself,

is a product of your choice and choices are so important. To a great extent, they determine the flavour of our lives.

On the other hand, the family into which you are born is not a product of your choice. The relationship between children and parents is established by birth. You do not choose who your father or mother would be before you are born. Or did you? You cannot change your father, neither can you change your mother. Nonetheless, the good news is that God never makes mistakes. Whatever family you are born into is not accidental; God did it on purpose, and it is for your good. Don't ever wish you were born into another family. The family into which you are born is the best for you to fulfil your reason for existence. Get excited! You are born in due season.

I am born into a family of ten: eight children, with me as the sixth. So divinely positioned by God, I am so grateful to Him for that. We are all born again and Spirit filled. Oh, what a sweet place to belong! Each of us eight children are now grown and mature. We have all left home, are married, and are now building our own families.

Don't ever despise the family into which you were born. No matter the challenges there, God might have sent you there for such a time as this. As you handle those challenges effectively, you will emerge a champion.

Fourthly, marriage is the foundation for the family. A marriage is entered into by choice and then grows into a family unit. The principles that keep the marriage standing, must flow into the lifestyle of family members. This is because in a marriage, an individual makes a choice for him/herself. But in establishing a family, the individual is bringing loved ones and more individuals together, to partake of the either healthy environment created or painful experiences being endured (Gen. 47:9). Marriage and family is meant to be enjoyed, not endured. In her testimony, Mrs. Ubom said:

"I lived with a plague of marital tension for seventeen and half years; no permanent peace, no joy. It started right from after our wedding. I noticed it was like a plague. I came to know the Lord, and He brought me to this place. I contacted the word of God and told God that I couldn't live with this marital tension.

To the glory of the Lord, in January, the Bishop talked about marriage dedication. Surprisingly, my husband said, 'What do you think about it?' I told him that we should go for it. And since that day (January 26th, 1997), to the glory of God, I'm free from tension!"

Living as a Family

After marriage comes the marital life or the life

experience of a couple. They no more live like single individuals. Changes have occurred and are still occurring. Each party has to now consider his/her partner and not only him/herself.

After the marriage, children are added (either by birth or adoption) and additional parties (related either by blood or association) come into the home. A family is then established. Families are products of marriages. One leads to the other.

Family

A family is a group of people affiliated by blood and / or marriage. It is the nucleus unit of the Church and a nation. It is a fundamental social group in society, typically consisting of a man and woman (known as husband and wife) and their offspring.

Whereas, a family consist of a group of persons sharing common ancestry, marriage consists of a man and a woman, known as husband and wife, who share common goals and values, have a long-term commitment to one another, and live together.

Family Life

Family life is the manner of living of a group of people who share common ancestry. It is the manner of living in a household, the manner of living of a group of people

21

affiliated by blood and marriage. It is the way in which parents, children, and close relations live.

Incidentally, no individual on earth, whether married or single, dropped from heaven. Every one on earth, young or old, rich or poor, male or female, black or white, came from one family or another, from one lineage or another, are connected to one person or the other genetically or by association. Issues on family and family life, therefore, affect everyone on earth.

The Family Structure

For every house is builded by some man; but he that built all things is God.

Hebrews 3:4

Every wise woman buildeth her house ...

Proverbs 14:1

The word "house" in the above passages is not referring to a physical structure, but to a family structure – the individuals who make up the home. It is man's responsibility to build his/her house. You build by organizing and administering the individuals under your roof.

Let the deacons be the husband of one wife, ruling (administering) their children and their own houses well.

1Timothy 3:12

The family structure requires effective administration.

When this is lacking, families in turn produce individuals who tear down and destroy the society. The essence of the family, therefore, is to create an atmosphere or environment for effective administration and preparation of individuals, so they can grow and properly pursue the plan of God for their lives.

Mrs. Graham, mother of the famous Tele-Evangelist, Billy Graham, speaking about family life said:

"...The house of the wicked shall be overthrown: but the tabernacle of the upright shall flourish ... There is a generation that curseth their father, and doth not bless their mother (Prov. 14:11; 30:11).

Mr. Graham and I did not want that to happen in our family. When we get away from what the Bible says, we are in trouble. We knew there was only one right way to live, and it was all laid out for us in the Bible. It is how we tried to live, and how we wanted our children to learn to live."

Billy Graham himself said, "In many crusades over the years, I have devoted at least one message to the subject of the family. In my depression-era growing up years we had family solidarity, we cared about each other, and we liked to do things together. My mother saw to it that we gathered frequently and regularly. She gathered us around herself and my father, to listen to Bible stories, to join in family prayers, and to share a sense of the presence of God."

No wonder the Grahams have an enviable family life. Your own testimony will be brighter, in Jesus name!

"Charity", they say, "begins at home." It doesn't end there though; it only begins from there. This means the home is where the character and destiny of an individual should begin and take proper shape. A typical biblical example of this is the case of Abraham. In Genesis 18:19, God speaking about Abraham said:

> *For I know him, that he will command his children and his household after him, and they shall keep the way of the Lord, to do justice and judgment; that the Lord may bring upon Abraham that which he hath spoken of him.*

Abraham had a grasp of God's purpose for the family, and by that understanding was able to order his household aright. The result of that was that God was pleased with him and ensured that Abraham and his household were successful in all that they did. Till today, Christians the world over still identify with Abraham. If God were to comment on your marriage or family today, would He say something positive about it?

The *family* is the foundational block for the society, while *marriage* is the foundational block for the family. Satan always targets marriages to destroy them. This is because to destroy marriages would mean to destroy families, and to destroy families would mean to destroy the Church, the society, and the nation. But we must not allow this to happen.

God established the family as the first and most fundamental element of the human society. Marriage is a foundational institution that existed before all other institutions. It is the oldest institution in the world. God is a God of priorities. He established the institution of marriage before the Church. He first set up marriage, before He came down to fellowship with man in the cool of the day (Gen. 2:18-25; 3:8).

Before there were nations or governments, schools or businesses, there was the family; and before the family was marriage. Marriage is foundational; it is on this relationship that God began to build society.

When God brought Adam and Eve together in the garden, marriage was the framework for the development of their social interaction as they grew together. It was in the context of marriage that they learned their responsibilities towards each other and lived out their commitments to each other. The human society in all its forms depends on the institution of marriage for survival.

Marriage is also the foundation upon which the Church, the community of believers, and God's special society rests. The New Testament describes the relationship between Christ and His Church, as being like that of a bridegroom and his bride. This analogy has significant implications for understanding how husbands and wives are to relate with each other (Eph. 5:21-23, 25, 31-32). The relationship between Christ and His Church is a model of what should exist between a husband and his wife: a relationship of respect, mutual submission and sacrificial love. All through the Bible, from Genesis to Revelation, the word "house" is used to refer to the family, the smallest, but yet the most basic unit of society. More than ever before, the family needs the help of God to be free from the troubles, woes, and calamities that befall it daily.

Although, every house and family is built by some man or woman, for any house or family to remain standing and stand the test of time, an understanding of what the family stands for must be grasped. Also, each family must be founded and built on the principles and master plan of God, the originator.

2

God's Master Plan For The Family

"And look that thou make them after their pattern, which was shewed thee in the mount."

Exodus 25:40

Attempting to put up any physical structure, without a master plan, will certainly end in futility. Once a master plan is drawn, all the builders have to do, is follow it explicitly, to end up with a beautiful building. The master plan is, therefore, the "map" of a building.

Marriage can be likened to a house. The Architect who drew the master plan is God, while the husband and his wife are the builders, who must diligently follow the design of the Architect, so as to experience success in their marriage and family. This is why the scriptures expressly says:

For every house is builded by some man; but he that

27

built all things is God.

Hebrews 3:4

Through wisdom is an house builded; and by understanding it is established.

Proverbs 24:3

The Plan

God's plan for marriage as an institution and the family is clearly stated in His word. This plan has to be discovered, understood and applied before the success inherent in it, can be enjoyed. Genesis 2:24 makes this abundantly clear:

Therefore shall a man leave his father and his mother, and shall cleave unto his wife and they shall be one flesh.

Three principles stand out clearly here: Leave, Cleave, and One Flesh. A discovery, understanding and application of these principles will make family success a reality. Let's examine each of them briefly.

Leave

The first principle in God's master plan involves leaving home. It is a command. When a man and his wife come together in marriage, they form a new family unit; separate and different from the ones each of them are coming from.

> *Therefore shall a man leave his father and his*
> *mother...*
>
> Genesis 2:24

Though the husband is specifically instructed about leaving in this scripture, the instruction includes the wife as well. This is because, until both of them succeed in leaving their respective homes, they cannot establish their new one. Also, the above instruction is very specific. It clearly states that a man should leave his father and mother, not sisters, brothers, uncles or aunts. Why? This is because father and mother are one's closest blood relations. If it is possible to leave them, it should be much more possible to easily leave brothers, sisters, uncles, aunts or any other relation.

The relationship between a husband and wife is permanent and should not be broken; but the one between parent and child is temporary, and, therefore, may be broken.

What then does it mean to leave? Leaving in this context means to gain parental independence. The day-to-day running of the new home should not be the concern of father, mother and relations. Rather, it should be left absolutely in the hands of the husband and his wife. It does not mean having nothing to do with parents anymore, but it does mean to operate as a separate and distinct family. It means disallowing the new family from being remotely controlled by the old ones they both are coming from. This should cover all areas of life. This principle is a fundamental one.

Physically, the man and his wife should leave. After marriage, the ideal thing is for a man and his wife to move into their own house, whether it is rented, leased or built by them. No matter how small the house, the size is not as important as the obedience to God's word. Even if it is only one room to start with, it is usually better. This makes the adjustment period easier for the man and his wife. They are able to live much easier as mature, independent adults. This is because both of them require time to be alone together, in order to know each other better.

A situation where a man and his wife after marriage still live in the same house physically with either parent, should be avoided as much as possible. In most cases, it strains relationships. A couple living in a one-room apartment today, has a potential of living in a mansion tomorrow. Never despise the days of small beginnings!

Emotionally, the man and his wife are meant to leave. God created us with emotions. It is important, however, to be able to give our emotions correct direction. By birth, children are emotionally attached to their parents. This emotional attachment to parents must be adequately handled after marriage, to avoid emotional breakdowns. Maturity is required here. This again suggests, why marriage in God's master plan is for the matured; for men and women only, not boys and girls.

Mentally, the husband and his wife should leave their parents. The man and his wife should be ready to take decisions on their own and accept responsibility for them. Life is all about responsibility! Both of them must be ready to rub minds together in decision making. They must be ready to face the challenges of life together. Decisions that directly affect their new family, should not be left for their parents to make for them. The blame for any decision that does not work, should not be passed onto their parents either. Some couples cannot take any step in life without the approval of their parents. This ought not to be. They both must leave mentally.

Financially also, a husband and his wife are expected to leave their parents. They ought to be financially independent. They must both be able to work, earn money and be financially responsible. They should not be a financial burden on their parents, neither should their parents be a financial burden on them.

To leave financially, husband and wife must learn to be contented with each phase of their lives. Life is in phases, and men are in sizes, my husband often says.

A word of caution here though! Without prejudice to all the above, a husband and his wife must ensure they fulfill their covenant obligations to their parents. Remember what Ephesians 6:2-3 says:

> *Honour thy father and mother; which is the first commandment with promise;*
>
> *That it may be well with thee, and thou mayest live long on the earth.*

Honour must be given to whom it is due. Learn to honour your parents. Honour is a seed. What you sow, you reap. When you become a parent, you reap what you sowed to your own parents. Life is give and take. To reap honour in your future, you must sow honour seeds today!

Cleave

Remember the foundation scripture for this section?

> *Therefore shall a man leave his father and his mother, and shall cleave unto his wife ...*
>
> -Genesis 2:24

The next principle in God's master plan for a successful marriage and family is cleaving. What does it mean to cleave?

The American Heritage Dictionary defines the word "cleav"e as "to adhere, cling, or stick fast to." In the light of this definition, in God's master plan, husbands and wives, are meant to adhere, cling, and stick fast to each other for life!

To cleave also means "joined to." This does not mean to glue both of them together physically. It means a coming together, a blending of two distinct individuals into one. This is why the scripture says in Ephesians 5:31:

> *For this cause shall a man leave his father and mother, and shall be joined unto his wife, and they two shall be one flesh.*

A man and his wife who had hitherto lived as two separate, distinct individuals, come into marriage; leaving father and mother, they cleave to each other for the rest of their lives. So then, they are no more two separate and distinct individuals, but now joined to one another. This is the basis for a life-long fellowship, friendship and relationship!

The effect of this is togetherness, closeness, and intimacy. It brings about unity. It produces oneness; oneness in all things – spirit, soul, and body. Oneness in spirit means both of them being spiritually alive, belonging to the same spiritual kingdom. Oneness in the realm of the soul means both of them being agreeable, in spite of their individual differences. Oneness in the realm of the body refers to their physical union as husband and wife, which is their creative power. And, wow, when united, nothing can be restrained from you (Gen. 11:6)! What a secret! Husbands and wives must, therefore, beware of whatever can bring division between them and give it no place.

Quarrels, rancour, bitterness, division, misunderstanding, malice, hatred and the likes must not be allowed, because they can put a husband and his wife apart, though still living under the same roof. A kingdom divided against itself cannot stand. Can you imagine a home where one spouse has deep-seated ill wishes towards the other spouse? Such a home will be a conducive place for the devil to operate. Of course, if you give the devil a place, he will take you away from your place. God is not the author of confusion. Wherever there is confusion, there is every evil work (Jms. 3:16).

I must say at this point, however, that there can be no cleaving until there is first a leaving. One must precede the other. Leaving comes before cleaving. God is a God of order and priorities. Until a man and his wife both leave their respective families from where they came, it will be impossible for them to cleave to each other.

Worthy of note also, is the fact that leaving does not guarantee cleaving. Cleaving is not automatic. It is possible to leave without cleaving. This is what results in loneliness, which is one of the major challenges in homes today. Loneliness has led to divisions, separations, and eventual divorce in many marriages.

Cleaving does not just happen because two people get into marriage. It must never be assumed. Rather, it has to be programmed for and deliberately worked at to make it happen. Effective communication is a vital, indispensable key in making this happen. This subject will be addressed later in this book.

One Flesh

This is the third principle in God's master plan.

...And they shall be one flesh.

Genesis 2:24

Wherefore they are no more twain, but one flesh...

Matthew 19:6

...And they two shall be one flesh.

Ephesians 5:31

In God's eyes, a husband and his wife are one flesh! This must be the reason why Adam, when he first saw his wife, said in Genesis 2:23:

"...This is now bone of my bones, and flesh of my flesh: she shall be called Woman, because she was taken out of Man."

One man and one woman, in a marriage relationship equal one flesh. This is God's arithmetic! This is referring to a fusion of husband and wife, two distinct elements into one. At this point, they become inseparable; cannot be "disjoined" anymore. It has become a permanent and life long relationship. This is nothing but a great mystery! The word of God attests to this in Ephesians 5:32.

A mystery is a truth that is incomprehensible to the reasoning, and is knowable only through divine revelation; something that baffles human understanding. When you understand, apply and live by the mysteries of God, you command mastery on the earth. The mysteries of God concerning marriage, when understood and applied, makes you overcome every marital misery!

The unique relationship between husband and wife is a mystery. The mystery of marriage is that two people from different backgrounds, having different will powers, likes and dislikes can come together in a life-long relationship, and adapt, blend and complement one another. This is difficult to explain, but is real.

God has not ordained marriage to bring misery, but to help free man from every form of misery, so he can gain mastery in life. As you follow God's master plan concerning marriage, I see your freedom from every misery in life established, and see you gain mastery, in Jesus' name! The following testimony is a proof.

"I have been married for ten years, and since then there

has been no peace in the home. For me, marriage wasn't good. Things were just upside down. I had a child in 1993 that died. Apart from that, I had series of miscarriages. I used to drive a car, but it was no more. It was as if everything came to a halt.

My husband started coming to Winners' Chapel in January 1997. He didn't ask me to come with him, because I was already attending another Pentecostal church. Yet, there was no peace in the home. The situation got worse, and in June last year, the tension was so high that I asked, 'Lord, what will I do?'

I told my husband, 'If this is what marriage is all about, let us call it quits.' He replied, 'The door is wide open, you can go.'

It was then I sat down and did a rethink. I came to Winners' Chapel in June, and I began to hear the Bishop say, 'I have been married for many years now and there has not been any concern or problem in my home.' I said to myself, 'Is it on this earth or in another planet?'

But somehow, God has done it for me! Now I know I had been the problem, not my husband. My husband is a perfect gentleman. The Bishop's wife jokingly says if there was anything as another life, she would still choose to marry her husband. I too can joyfully say the same thing today!"

— **Neburabo, R. (Mrs.)**

The Mystery of One Flesh

There are so many things to learn from this. Let's examine some of them.

Treat Your Spouse As Yourself

An understanding of the mystery of one flesh will make husband and wife treat each other the same way. What you cannot do to yourself, don't do to your spouse. Treat your spouse the way you want your spouse to treat you. Care for your spouse the same way you want him/her to care for you.

If you want your spouse to be kind to you, then you have a responsibility to be kind, not cruel to him/her. If you want to be respected by your spouse, do same first. What you sow, is what you reap. Do not maltreat your spouse, if you do not want to be maltreated in return. What you put into marriage is what it will give back to you!

> *For no man ever yet hated his own flesh; but nourisheth and cherisheth it, even as the Lord the church.*
>
> Ephesians 5:29

The American Heritage Dictionary defines **"nourish"** as "to provide with food or other substances necessary for life and growth; feed. To foster the development of, promote." It defines "cherish" as "treat with affection and tenderness; hold dear. To keep fondly in mind."

A husband and wife should foster the development of each other, promote each other, treat each other with affection and tenderness, hold each other dear, and keep each other fondly in mind. It takes an understanding of the mystery of one flesh to be able to do this.

To love your spouse is to love yourself, and to hate your spouse is to hate yourself. Some couples so maltreat each other that they physically beat each other. But an understanding and application of the mystery of one flesh can terminate this misery, just as it did for the sister in this testimony:

"My husband deserted my two children and me, and stopped giving us feeding allowance. He would even beat me whenever he was in town.

At a time, he didn't come home for six months. I got to know where he was from the company calendar, and when I got there, he said he didn't tell me to come. He left me there for three days! I started seeking help from everywhere I could think of – both from churches and ungodly avenues. But things just got worse!

Then an elderly couple invited me to this church. I was touched when the Bishop's wife ministered on forgiveness and forgetting the past, and I prayed.

Thereafter, things turned around completely! My husband returned and asked for forgiveness. My marriage is now restored and there is now peace in my home."

— **Philips, T. (Mrs.)**

Make No Provision For Divorce.

Do all within your power to avoid divorce.

> **For the LORD, the God of Israel, saith that he hateth putting away: for one covereth violence with his garment, saith the LORD of hosts: therefore take heed to your spirit, that ye deal not treacherously.**
>
> Malachi 2:16

God hates putting away! What God hates, you should hate too. What God has joined together, nothing should put asunder (Matt. 19:5-6; Mk.10:9).

When there is a challenge in your home, divorce should not be the first option that comes to mind. Rather, it is important to first identify and analyze the challenge. Then, make proposals and choose a possible solution. This way, most problems can be solved.

What you don't confront you never conquer. Be committed to deal with problems, not walk away from them. If you sleep with problems, you will still wake up to meet them the next day!

Divorce can be likened to marital amputation. It

causes a lot of grief, pain, and wound that only God can heal. Even when a wound is healed, the scar remains, and in most cases, for life. Make no plans for divorce. Remember, prevention is said to be better than cure.

When part of a man's body is amputated, even when an artificial replacement is in place, the difference is still there. People who see such a man from afar off may not notice that a part of his body has been amputated, but he that is concerned cannot claim ignorance!

See what the word says:

> *...Moses because of the hardness of your hearts suffered you to put away your wives: but from the beginning it was not so.*
>
> Matthew 19:8

> *And unto the married I command, yet not I, but the Lord, Let not the wife depart from her husband ...and let not the husband put away his wife.*
>
> I Corinthians 7:10-11

So, divorce was not part of God's plan for marriage from the beginning. One of the greatest tragedies of our days, is the many marriages that end up in divorce. Divorce is always tragic and traumatic. The breakdown of the family unit, is one of the greatest calamities our society faces today. The partners go through untold agonies, not to talk of the shattered lives of children, who go through turmoil and devastation. God views husbands and wives as having been bound together in a permanent marriage relationship, and nothing should be allowed to put them asunder.

Probably, you are reading this book and have been considering divorce, according to you because there is no way out. Hold it! Who knows, this might be the reason God gave you the opportunity of reading this book. If only you accept and follow God's master plan, your story will change for the better.

Or, are you already divorced? Do not allow a sense of condemnation to overwhelm and destroy your colorful future. God is a restorer. Do you know a miracle can still take place in your life and family to bring about a restoration? God is a restorer! Someone sent me this testimony sometime ago.

"I read your article in the newspaper. In fact, I have seen a lot of changes in my life, which prompted me to give this glorious testimony of the wonderful works of our Lord Jesus Christ.

I got married in 1977 as an unbeliever, before I joined the police force in the year 2000. But somehow, the marriage broke up as a result of so many things. But God rebuilt the marriage from the advice and instruction I got from your article.

I congratulate you for your effort in enlightening young men and women concerning their marital lives, so that their marriages will be peaceful and successful.

— **Mr. Udual, A. (Awka)**

And I will restore to you the years that the locust hath eaten, the cankerworm, and the caterpillar, and the palmerworm ...

Joel 2:25

God will give you a glorious testimony too!

The general principle is: no divorce. But if you are already divorced, God picks you up where you are. If you are re-married now, God recognises the marriage relationship you are in now, as binding. What you did in the past is past, ask God for forgiveness and go on from there. How you got into this present marriage not withstanding, it is the one God wants you to stay in now. You need to make it a biblical relationship.

Sometime ago, I read a research finding where it was stated that divorced people generally die younger than those who stay married. You shall not die young; rather you shall fulfill the number of your days! It pays to stay away from divorce, and you are the one to benefit if you do.

Now, let me make it clear at this point that God is a God of a second chance. If you have to or have gone through divorce, do not live life with a sense of condemnation. Straighten things out with God and with men. Make sure that your present marital status is such that will not rob you of eternity with God. With this, you are set to make the most of life.

Share Your Bodies With One Another

Husbands and wives should learn to share their physical bodies with one another. After marriage, the physical body of the husband belongs to the wife, and that of the wife belongs to the husband. Both of them are to enjoy satisfaction from each other's body. They are not expected to refrain their bodies from one another anymore. The scripture says in I Corinthians 7:4-5:

> *The wife hath not power of her own body, but the husband: and likewise also the husband hath not power of his own body, but the wife.*
>
> *Defraud ye not one the other...*

Man and wife, understand that your physical union is your creative power. God created sex, and it is a key part of our lives. It is meant to be enjoyed exclusively by a husband and his wife after marriage. This physical union is what produces children. Sex is to be enjoyed, not endured. Don't use it to punish your spouse!

In marriage, sex is the ultimate in oneness between a husband and wife. Your sex life affects your attitude positively or negatively. Sexual tension is the foundation of crises in many marriages and homes, but it can be avoided. My husband says, when a marriage lacks romance it starts suffering disintegration. God invented sex for the exclusive enjoyment of the husband and wife. The Bible is a book about sex. It talks honestly about the human sex drive and is more forthright on it than many recently published manuals (Judg. 14:1-2). After all, it was naked Eve that God brought to naked Adam! Husband and wife should, therefore, not be ashamed of each other's nakedness.

Sex in marriage is purely an act of giving, so it should be used only in its proper place and time, according to God's master plan. For everything original, there is a counterfeit. Satan seeks to pervert sex. Husband and wife use your body with your spouse correctly, not with an ill or selfish motive. For example, never give your body to your spouse because you want to get something from him/her. In marriage, never be found prostituting your body; it is perverted sex!

When a husband and wife are truly united in body, it becomes easy to overcome temptations from outside. Remember that sex is only proper in the context of marriage. Outside of marriage, sex is sin (I Cor. 6:9). In actual fact, it is the scarlet sin, and it sinks destinies! Your destiny shall not sink!

So then, if you follow God's master plan concerning marriage, you will surely enjoy success inspite of the devil. God designed marriage and family life to be successful. The marriage relationship is meant to be one of joy and mutual fulfillment. Right from biblical days, men and women have enjoyed their marriages and families.

You may say, however, judging by your experience and that of people around you, that every family has its own problems. Nothing can be farther from the truth. For instance, that you have headache does not necessarily mean that everyone else has it. It is quite possible to have a hitch-free family life here on earth. Searching the scriptures, I found evidences of people who had hitch-free family lives by their testimonies and encounters to back up my claim. Let's see some of them briefly:

NOAH

And the LORD said unto Noah, Come thou and all thy house into the ark; for thee have I seen righteous before me in this generation.

Genesis 7:1 (emphasis mine)

After the fall of man, Noah's family was the first to distinguish itself in an evil generation. He was such a successfully married man that God singled him and all members of his family out in the midst of destruction.

It is amazing to know that a man can succeed in family life even before the dispensation of grace. That is to say that even before the coming of Jesus and the era of grace, a man had won God's favour by his commitment to his family.

But Noah found grace in the eyes of the LORD.

Genesis 6:8

If Noah could make it, then you and I have no excuse to fail in our families. There is no reason for pressure, tension, or frustration in your family, because Jesus already paid the price in full. He was our perfect substitute. He was wounded, bruised, beaten, humiliated, spat on, etc, so that we may enjoy glory and honour in our homes. That is why no man has any excuse for beating his wife. None whatsoever! It takes a man who is not in his right mind to beat himself. In the same vein, because a husband and his wife are one flesh, only a man who is not in his right mind will physically beat his spouse in marriage (Mk.10:8)

ABRAHAM

For I know him, that he will command his children and his household after him, and they shall keep the way of the LORD, to do justice and judgment; that the LORD may bring upon Abraham that which he hath spoken of him.

Genesis 18:19

47

Abraham the father of nations was also a very successful married man. In those days when the law had not been delivered, Abraham remained faithful to his barren wife. Even before he became the friend of God, he had a successful marriage. His relationship with and closeness to God did not reduce his commitment to his family; rather, it enhanced it.

He was a man God could count on to command his family to follow after Him. If truly we are children of Abraham, it should be for us "like father, like son." That's why Isaiah 51:2 says:

> *Look unto Abraham your father, and unto Sarah that bare you: for I called him alone, and blessed him, and increased him.*

It is time to look like and act as our father, Abraham; not only for a life of faith, but also faithfulness in building our families following God's blueprint. Tell yourself that if Abraham did not have problems in his family life then you too would not. It is about time you started walking in the footsteps of your father. If Abraham made it, so will you!

PETER

> *And when Jesus was come into Peter's house, he saw his wife's mother laid, and sick of a fever.*

And he touched her hand, and the fever left her:
and she arose, and ministered unto them.

Matthew 8:14-15

Simon Peter, one of the foremost apostles and right-hand man to Jesus during His earthly walk, was a successful married man. There is no reason to doubt that Peter was successfully married, because there is no record of any day his wife or any of his children came to the crusade ground to challenge him for not fulfilling his marital obligations!

I believe one major reason he could fulfill his course with joy, was because he had peace at home. His marriage was not an obstacle to his ministry or vice versa. Ministers of the gospel need to learn a lesson here. Ministry work is not an acceptable excuse for a dysfunctional marriage or family. If Peter could make it inspite of the tight schedule Jesus ran, no one has an acceptable reason to fail.

These are proofs that success in family life is a reality, and only fools doubt proofs. We, therefore, have a responsibility to apply ourselves to the principles of God's word, which is the blue print for marital success. With this understanding of God's master plan, get set to begin constructing a successful family life, free from failure, pressure, shame and unproductivity.

3

Why Family Success?

Success in anything in life, and particularly in marriage, is not accidental. It is a product of proper alignment with the truth of God's word. No accident is ever said to be successful. No one succeeds by chance. A successful marriage does not just happen; it is made to happen. A wise man said, "Many people dream of success, but others wake up and work at it!" The responsibility for the success of your family rests absolutely on you, and that begins with your perception of the family.

There is a purpose for every existing thing; and the family is no exception. Purpose is power! When the purpose for the family is clearly understood, then proper family structure and values will be upheld, treasured and strengthened.

A lack of understanding of and appreciation for what the family is and what it stands for, ultimately creates a tendency for abuse, misuse, and the taking for granted of this important institution, which serves as the foundation for every nation and people.

Why Create Families?

Why the family? What is the reason for its existence?

For every house is builded by some man...

Hebrews 3:4

God's purpose for the family is seen in the above scripture: *"every house is builded by some man."* Families and households are relationships meant for building the individual members. There is a building process that is meant to take place in the lives of the individuals that make up a family or household. The family is the God-ordained environment for such building process. However, faulty family foundations have resulted in family members being partially built up; half baked individuals, which always result in societal and national decadence.

There are values to be taught, as well as character traits to be imbibed among family members, and the family environment is the God-ordained place for such training. Without a proper understanding of what the family and home is meant to be (a place and environment for building godly and strong character in the individuals, a place to build individuals ready to render loving and selfless service), that house or family cannot be built up, neither can that nation be established. The Lord Jesus said,

> *A house divided against itself cannot stand.*
>
> Matthew 12:25

It is so important that you have a clear picture of what the family stands for, that you see what the originator (God) had in mind when He created it. This understanding will help you appraise your own family.

We have seen how the Bible uses the word "house" to refer to the smallest and most basic unit of the society –the family. We have also established that the house is the foundation of any society, and that marriage is what forms the initial foundation for every house. This means that the health of any nation or society, is determined by the health of the families in that nation, and the health of the families in that nation is determined by the health of the marriage relationships such families are founded on.

Successful and solid families don't just come into existence. In order for them to be properly built up, they must be established on a proper marriage foundation. The proper foundation involves first a bonding between two people- a man and a woman, after which children are born. The practice of children being born out of wedlock, abandoned babies, the co-habitation of unmarried men and women, or people of the same sex is not a proper foundation to build a family on.

God's word warns against improper foundation. Look at this scripture:

> *If the foundations be destroyed, what can the righteous do?*
>
> Psalm 11:3

If the family foundation is faulty, then the result you will get will be faulty people in society, that will eventually lead all to misery.

Every Christian couple should aspire to succeed in their marriage and family life, even though some think it is actually no one's business whether they make it or not in marriage. That is erroneous, especially because the success or failure of a family, particularly a Christian family, has far greater effects than many couples know.

Must The Family Succeed?

How can we be sure that God designed the family to succeed? Let's examine this subject briefly.

The Lord God Caused...

> *And the Lord God caused a deep sleep to fall upon Adam, and he slept: and took one of his ribs, and closed up the flesh instead thereof;*
>
> *And the rib, which the Lord God had taken from*

man, made he a woman, and brought her unto the man.

Genesis 2:21-22

This account in the book of Genesis is the account of the very first wedding ceremony. God was practically involved in the institution of the first family unit ever. God did not just speak it into existence, like He did the rest of creation, He made Adam. He caused him to sleep a deep sleep, and then took a rib from his side. Out of this rib, He formed the woman and brought her unto Adam.

God Himself, therefore, was the initiator. This means then that marriage is rooted in divinity. Without any doubt, anything associated with God is meant to succeed. Marriage is associated with God, therefore, it is meant to be successful.

He said, **"Be fruitful..."**

So God created man in his own image, in the image of God created he him; male and female created he them.

And God blessed them, and God said unto them, Be fruitful, and multiply, and replenish the earth, and subdue it: and have dominion over the fish of the sea, and over the fowl of the air, and over every living thing that moveth upon the earth.

Genesis 1:27-28

God began the human family by blessing, not cursing it. He said to Adam and Eve, "Be fruitful; multiply; replenish the earth; subdue it!" What wonderful words of blessing!

Fruitfulness goes beyond procreation; it includes success in all areas of life. It also means having many good results. The fact that God rained blessings on the first family, is a clear indication that every family is meant to be successful. These blessings will answer for you, in Jesus' name!

Have Dominion...!

...Have dominion over the fish of the sea, and over the fowl of the air, and over every living thing that moveth upon the earth.

-Genesis 1:28

The American Heritage Dictionary defines "dominion" as "control or the exercise of control." The family was established, therefore, to have dominion; that is, to have and exercise control. It was established to be in control of, and not under the control of circumstances and situations of life. This in itself is a sign that it was established for success.

He Put Them In Eden

And the LORD God took the man, and put him into

the Garden of Eden to dress it and to keep it.

Genesis 2:15

It is evident that the family was designed for success, because of the place where God placed them. If you have read the description of Eden, you will appreciate the fact that Eden was no wilderness. In fact, it literally means delight, or great pleasure.

God placed the first couple in a place of pleasure. His desire is that your family gives you pleasure. All family members should enjoy one another, experience fulfillment, laughter and excitement. He never intended the family to experience pressure, but pleasure. He designed the family to make life pleasurable. In case the situation in your family is far from being pleasant, as you read this book, believe God for a reversal, and it shall be so for you!

They Were Not Ashamed

And they were both naked, the man and his wife, and were not ashamed.

Genesis 2:25

God instituted marriage to ensure that man never experienced shame. Marriage brought man into a state of better living, glory, and beauty. There was no cause for fear or regret.

The third reason God instituted the family, and one of many reasons He designed it for success, is to take shame away from you. You will not see shame anymore!

This Beginning of Miracles...

This beginning of miracles did Jesus in Cana of Galilee, and manifested forth his glory; and his disciples believed on him.

John2:11

It is absolutely awesome to discover that the first miracle ever performed by Jesus during His earthly ministry, was at a wedding ceremony. God is a God of priorities, who would always put first things first. By this miracle, He put a stamp of approval on the need for success in the family.

At this particular wedding, the wine had finished. The wine here represents joy. Jesus then stepped in, instructed them on what to do, they obeyed and thus had more wine than at the onset of the wedding.

The family is ordained of God to be a miracle centre! Many have and are still enjoying miracles in their marriages and families; yours will be the next! Read this testimony:

"Two years ago, I had problems in my marriage, and it eventually broke up. A sister invited me here, and since I started coming and hearing the wisdom of God, my

marriage has now been restored. My husband is even here in church; he is a WOFBI (Word of Faith Bible Institute) June Special student!"

This teaches that obedience to God's word brings sustained joy and fulfillment into a marriage. It also removes shame. Your shame is over, and the time for your miracle is here!

Consequences Of A Bad Marriage

What then are the consequences of a bad marriage? What happens when a couple does not succeed in their marriage?

Your Christian Testimony Is Affected

For the name of God is blasphemed among the Gentiles through you...

Romans 2:24

When a Christian family fails, it gives unbelievers room to blaspheme the name of God. When your unbelieving neighbours hear you and your wife fighting and quarreling everyday, calling your children all manner of ungodly names, or your children are typical examples of what the Bible refers to as "unruly", your Christian testimony is actually what is being affected. How will you witness to them or invite them to church, when they are aware of the situation in your family? There is nothing to emulate in your family.

As a man, if you shy away from your covenant responsibilities in the home –such as the provision of basic necessities of life, how do you expect the unbelievers around you to accept your Christian testimony? If a man travels out of town just at the point when his wife is about to put to bed or his children are about to resume at school, making no provisions whatsoever for them, what kind of testimony does he have? These affect his Christian testimony negatively.

It Hinders Answers to Prayers

> *"Likewise, ye husbands, dwell with them according to knowledge, giving honour unto the wife, as unto the weaker vessel, and as being heirs together of the grace of life; that your prayers be not hindered."*
>
> 1 Peter 3:7

Disharmony in a Christian home, is the fastest way to hinder you from receiving answers to prayer. Remember that prayer is essentially, communication with God. When your family is in disarray, try as you may, your prayer will be hindered.

Every Christian requires that special relationship with God that is cultivated, as we spend time in communion with Him. But when you and your spouse or members of your household are always at loggerheads, not only your relationship with them is affected, your relationship with God is affected as well! Remember that God's eyes run to and fro the earth. So, He sees you when you are fighting with your spouse, after which you go to church to pray and fellowship. God is not mocked; He cannot be deceived.

As you straighten out your relationship with your family members, your communication line with God will not be blocked, in Jesus' name!

Your Giving is Unfruitful

"Therefore if thou bring thy gift to the altar, and there rememberest that thy brother hath ought against thee;

Leave there thy gift before the altar, and go thy way; first be reconciled to thy brother, and then come and offer thy gift."

Matthew 5:23-24

This explains why a lot of Christians give so much, yet receive so little! They quarrel and fight at home, and then bring their gifts to the altar and expect it to be fruitful. Giving is a futile exercise until there's sanctity in the home. God is not in need; even if He were, no human is qualified to meet His needs! We all depend on Him for sustenance.

Your first neighbour is your spouse and members of

your household. So, if you want God to honour your seeds sown, ensure you are at peace with your family. Until that is in place, your giving amounts to nothing.

The Future Of Your Children Is Affected

Family disharmony greatly affects the future of the children in such homes. This is primarily because for a child, "an ounce of example is worth much more than a ton of preachment," says a wise man.

Whenever you are quarreling and fighting, your children are taking note of it. One day, they will ask you whether you are genuinely born-again! On the other hand, you must also realise that whatever your marriage looks like could be duplicated in their homes in the future. Children at the end of the day, look like their parents. Would you want your children to be doing what you are doing now? That is a food for thought! Can you boldly ask your children to follow you as you follow God? Wouldn't they miss heaven if they were to follow your example?

Don't let your lack of commitment to the success of your family, become a hindrance to your children in the future. Those children may be small now, but they are the future generation. Never under-estimate your children; they know exactly what goes on in your bedroom late at night. Beware! May you leave a Christian legacy for your children; may they remember you for good!

In concluding this chapter, let me state very clearly that God designed marriage and family for success. For this success to become a reality, however, each marriage partner has parts to play. Man is the primary beneficiary of family success, not God. If your marriage succeeds, you are the one to benefit, and if it fails you are the one to suffer. You shall succeed!

4

Laying A Solid Foundation

"If the foundations be destroyed, what can the righteous do?"

Psalms 11:3

A building is only as good as its foundation. That is why some buildings collapse in spite of their beautiful architectural designs. Nothing can adequately substitute the need for a solid foundation. The family is not left out. Its success hinges on the quality of its foundation.

The period before the wedding can be regarded as the foundation-laying period for the family. The right choice of a life partner, the quality of the courtship, etc, all determine just how successful the marriage will be.

There are some very simple basic principles I shall be discussing here. Note, however, that in their simplicity is profundity. These principles cannot be overlooked, because success is not guaranteed without a firm grip on them. Let's examine them closely.

Marry A Christian

> *"Be ye not unequally yoked together with unbelievers: for what fellowship hath righteousness with unrighteousness? and what communion hath light with darkness?*
>
> *And what concord hath Christ with Belial? or what part hath he that believeth with an infidel?"*
>
> 2 Corinthians 6:14-15

Three words stand out clearly here: fellowship, communion, and concord. Let's briefly take a closer look at each of these words. Fellowship means to share similar interests, ideals or experiences. It means equals, sharing similar interests. Concord means harmony or agreement of interests or feeling. Communion means the act or an instance of sharing as of thoughts or feelings. These three words communicate a unique and clear message: "togetherness." You will find that these words – fellowship, communion, and concord summarize what marriage is all about.

Take these three components out of marriage, and it is doomed, because marriage is a mysterious union of two different individuals, who come together in a special covenant relationship. So, marriage is all about togetherness.

If family success is your goal as a Christian, you must ensure that you get married to a Christian. This way, you will be laying a solid foundation.

A saved person and an unbeliever cannot have real fellowship, communion or concord. This is primarily because there is a fundamental difference between the character and life of one who is saved and one who is not saved. I can hear someone ask, "How do I know the difference between them?" You know the difference by their fruits (Matt.7:20).

A personal relationship with Jesus is the cornerstone of any successful marriage (Col.1:13). There is no meeting point between a Christian and a sinner (Gen. 24:3). It is unbiblical for a Christian to marry a non-Christian.

Two people going into marriage must of necessity do so with someone in the same spiritual kingdom (Amos 3:3). Abraham the father of faith knew so well the importance of his son marrying from among his brethren and not from just anywhere. He commanded:

"But thou shalt go unto my country, and to my kindred, and take a wife unto my son Isaac."

Genesis 24:4

The Abrahamic covenant does not permit you to marry a stranger; it must be from among your brethren. We as children of Abraham must do likewise. There is a tendency for Christian men and women to succumb to social, financial, or parental pressures. But no matter where the pressure is coming from, you must make up your mind that nothing will drive you into a relationship with an unbeliever. That will be equal to building on a faulty foundation! Such a building will collapse like a pack of cards in no time. Beware!

Someone once asked me: "I am a Christian, and a young man has asked my hand in marriage. I know that he is not born again, can't I go ahead and marry him and believe that he will get born again after marriage?"

Don't be deceived to think that you can go ahead to marry an unbeliever with the intention of converting him or her after marriage; you are not the Holy Spirit! A Christian marrying a non-Christian is disobedience to God's word, and is equal to building on a faulty foundation.

In case you are a single Christian in a relationship with an unbeliever, you need to put a stop to it now, so it does not stop your destiny! Your destiny shall not be aborted! Never attempt to continue the relationship, saying to yourself, "I will just go to church and have the union blessed." You are courting trouble! You cannot mock God; what you sow is what you will reap (Gal. 6:7).

Christians must marry only Christians. It is a simple principle, but a very powerful one. There is a world of difference between the life of a Christian and that of an unbeliever. Both of them belong to two different kingdoms spiritually. The wealth and position of the man or woman in question notwithstanding, the fact remains: except you belong to the same spiritual kingdom, you are building your home on a faulty foundation.

In the following scriptures, we see how the wisest and richest king in Israel missed it at the end of his life, because he ignored this very important and fundamental principle.

> *"And Solomon's wisdom excelled the wisdom of all the children of the east country, and all the wisdom of Egypt.*
>
> *For he was wiser than all men; than Ethan the Ezrehite, and Heman, and Chalcol, and Darda, the sons of Mahol: and his fame was in all nations round about."*
>
> I Kings 4:30-31

> *"So king Solomon exceeded all the kings of the earth for riches and for wisdom."*
>
> I Kings 10:23

In 2 Chronicles 8:11, the Bible records that Solomon built a separate house for the daughter of Pharaoh, away from the City of David, because it was holy. That means Solomon knew that his union with Pharaoh's daughter was an unholy alliance.

> *"And Solomon brought up the daughter of Pharaoh out of the city of David unto the house that he built for her: for he said, My wife shall not dwell in the house of David king of Israel, because the places are holy, whereunto the ark of the Lord hath come."*

Just as expected, when Solomon was old, his wives turned his heart away from God. You need to take caution and beware! I Kings 11:4 says:

> *"For it came to pass, when Solomon was old, that his wives turned away his heart after other gods: and his heart was not perfect with the Lord his God, as was the heart of David his father."*

The story is told of a man, who spent all night praying, for God to put a seal of approval on his plan to marry an unbeliever. After the all-night service, the great man of God, Kenneth Hagin, asked him what he had been praying about. When he discovered what it was, he made it clear to the man that he needn't have wasted all night praying for something that is not God's will!

That is the problem with some believers; they want to make God approve what is contrary to His will. But

God cannot be manipulated. He will never approve what is contrary to His will. Whatever God does not approve is doomed from the onset.

Be A Successful Christian

Successful families are products of successful individuals. In Genesis 2: 19, the word of God says:

> *"And out of the ground the Lord God formed every beast of the field, and every fowl of the air; and brought them unto Adam to see what he would call them: and whatsoever Adam called every living creature, that was the name thereof."*

In essence, God first gave Adam an assignment, to see how successful he would be at it, before giving him a wife. Marriage is about responsibility. If Adam could not manage the responsibility of naming the animals, there was no guarantee that he could handle the added responsibility of a family. It was when Adam succeeded in that assignment that God added to him the gift, the favour, and blessing of a wife.

As an individual, you cannot succeed in marriage until you have succeeded as a single. For instance, if as a single you find it difficult to pray, study the word of God, attend fellowship or be of service in the kingdom; if your heart is not panting after God, the chances that you will develop these habits after marriage are slim.

This is especially true considering the fact that as a single your time is more or less at your own disposal; you do not have the added responsibility of caring for a family. So you can be more effective in the kingdom of God.

"But I would have you without carefulness. He that is unmarried careth for the things that belongs to the Lord, how he may please the Lord:

But he that is married careth for the things that are of the world, how he may please his wife."

1 Corinthians 7:32-33

Many Christians think that success in marriage is only predicated upon marrying the right person. Much more than this is the fact that family success is based on being the right person. Get serious with God, and be as good as the person you want to marry.

For instance, if you as a Christian brother want to marry a virgin, are you a virgin yourself? If as a Christian lady you want to marry a pastor, become a "pastor material." Remember that water will always seek its own level. Birds of the same feather, they say, flock together. Like always begets like. The kind of person you are determine the kind of person you attract.

No serious-minded believer will want to go into a relationship with an unserious Christian. Even if he or she sees a vision and hears a voice announcing you as his life partner, he may likely bind the devil and cast out that vision, because he knows your spiritual state.

It will amount to a waste of effort to keep praying and fasting for a God-fearing wife, "bombarding" the gates of heaven day and night, when you are unserious with God yourself. Make your ways right before God first, and He will simply add to you the blessing of a wife.

> *"But seek ye first the kingdom of God, and his righteousness; and all these things shall be added unto you."*
>
> Matthew 6:33

This was the platform upon which my husband stood to get a wife (me, of course!) When he discovered this scripture, he simply invested his life into the work of God, and God added a sweet home to him. Your own testimony will be sweeter!

The Platform For Your Choice

From my studies, I discovered that the basis upon which people make their choice for life partners is tri-dimensional: physical, soulish (emotional, intellectual) and spiritual. Once they sense a bonding or unity with someone in any or all these three areas, they believe that they have located their spouse. Let's take a brief look at each of these.

Unity Of The Flesh

This is a relationship that thrives on physical gratification. Some people get into marriage when they have a unity of the flesh or unity in the physical with someone. For example, you see a young man or woman and say, "Oh, he is handsome," or "Oh, she is beautiful. Look at her figure, look at her complexion." All that has attracted you is simply the physical appearance. While nothing is wrong with this realm of attraction in itself, it is a wrong premise on which to contract a life-long relationship.

What many people tend to forget is that people change over time. The man who is broad shouldered, flat-tummied, and all muscle today can become pot-bellied, flabby, and bald tomorrow. If your relationship is only based on the physical appearance of a person, your love will fade as his or her looks change. So then, this is not a strong enough foundation to keep husband and wife together for life. There is need for caution.

Unity Of The Soul

The second platform upon which many people decide on a mate is the soulish platform, which includes the emotions, intellect, and will. Perhaps you find a woman who reasons like you do. Both of you share the same interests in music, dance, drama, etc. So you think,

"Ah, may be she can make a good wife." You think both of you are "compatible."

In another scenario, you may meet someone, one look at the person, and you "fall" head-over-heels in "love". You develop strong feelings for the person, and decide to get married. Basing a relationship purely on the unity of the soul is risky, because likes and dislikes change overtime. The things you like doing today, you may find childish tomorrow, or you simply lose interest in later.

Then again, emotions are fickle. That's why you hear of people who fell in love and later fall out of love! Remember that even values change. Therefore, although it is essential to agree in your likes and dislikes, have similar interests, be emotionally attracted to one another, these should not be the primary reason for contracting a marriage.

Unity Of The Spirit

The most important unity that must exist between a man and a woman, which will also determine how much the marriage flourishes, is that of the spirit; and this can only happen between two born-again Christians, because outside Christ, all men are spiritually dead. When an individual is said to be born-again, it is his spirit which died in Adam that has now been re-born.

When there is unity of the spirit, there is an agreement in the fundamental spiritual matters listed in Hebrews 6:1-2. So, it is not just any Christian who will do. Find out also if you agree on certain fundamental principles and doctrinal issues.

> *"Therefore leaving the principles of the doctrine of Christ, let us go on unto perfection; not laying again the foundation of repentance from dead works, and of faith toward God,*
>
> *Of the doctrine of baptisms, and of laying on of hands, and of resurrection of the dead, and of eternal judgment."*
>
> Hebrews 6:1-2

In essence, do you agree on the following:

● Repentance from dead works

● Faith towards God

● The doctrine of baptisms (Holy Ghost and immersion by water)

● The laying on of hands (either for impartation or healing)

● The resurrection of the dead (or is he/she a Sadducee)

● Eternal judgment

And to add to that list:

76

- Are you heading in the same direction? Do you have a similar calling or vision?

- Are there other doctrines which his or her church subscribes to? Do you know them, and are you comfortable with them?

The most important of these dimensions is the spiritual, and I have found out that even when the physical and soulish are not 100% satisfactory, once the spiritual is intact, the others also find fulfillment. When you get married based on the unity of the spirit, you will find that the needs of the soul and the flesh are also wonderfully met!

Lester Sumrall described how he met his wife in one of his books I read sometime back. He said the first time he saw his wife, his flesh told him, "This lady is beautiful" (paraphrased). Then as they talked together, he noticed that they had many soulish things in common – they had the same mind on many issues of life. But the main reason he decided to marry her was her dedication, devotion, and unwavering love for the things of God. They were happily married for about 50 years before his wife went home to be with the Lord.

I also had a very similar experience. When I met my husband, I observed that he is a very handsome man. Something from within told me, "This is the man!" Not only that, we had (and still have) the same mind about various issues of life. But most importantly, what actually brought us together, and has helped us record the kind of success we enjoy in our marriage today, is the spiritual qualities he possessed: dedication and unwavering commitment to Christ and His kingdom.

And guess what? He was actually on a trip, on kingdom service when we met! It's been over thirty years since we first met and agreed to marry each other, and we have actually been married for about twenty-four years now, and it's still getting sweeter by the day!

Make Your Courtship Purposeful

Courtship is the period between when two people agree to marry and when they actually do. A successful courtship is a necessary step towards a successful marriage. The reason many people experience misunderstandings and all kinds of trouble in marriage is because they did not have a purposeful courtship.

There are certain factors that enhance the quality of your courtship.

Spend Time Talking Together

To ensure a qualitative courtship, you must create time to be with your fiancé(e), during which you share things about each other: your dreams, interests, view points, calling or assignment, etc. That is why it is important to spend time talking together, not just looking at each other and saying, "Oh you are so beautiful. I love you so much."

Your words are an indication of your thoughts and the direction in which you are going. If you want to know if he is a serious Christian, listen to him talk for five minutes. I discovered that it is impossible to separate an individual from his words.

If your fiancé(e), for instance, only talks about money, it is an indication that he or she is money minded. If on the other hand he is only interested in your physique, you will hear him speak of nothing else. Your words are an outflow of the thoughts of your heart.

"How can ye, being evil, speak good things? for out of the abundance of the heart the mouth speaketh."
Matthew 12:34

My husband and I courted for six years, and every time I heard him speak, I knew the direction he was heading. I knew his convictions, which were my convictions also. So, it became easy for both of us to flow together.

Appear in Public Together

This is another simple, but significant element. As intending couples, you must make out time to appear in public meetings together. Such public meetings may include, but are not limited to, the following: church services, weddings, matriculation and graduation ceremonies, public lectures, academic seminars, etc. I also advocate that as you appear together in public, watch how both of you conduct yourselves. How your partner-to-be responds to issues: his behaviour or reactions to annoying situations. This will be a signal of what the future holds. For instance, if he or she lacks Christian character, you are heading for trouble by going into marriage with such a person.

If you find out that for any social reason, such as height, age, educational differences, physical defects, personal carriage, eating manner, etc., you are ashamed to appear in public with your future husband or wife, and you don't handle it during courtship, you may never make a good couple. Be real and do not go through courtship with the eyes of your mind closed!

Courtship Should Have Letters

Every normal courtship should have letters. A letter is simply a written or printed communication directed to a person. One of the easiest ways to communicate during courtship is through letters. This becomes very handy, especially if the individuals involved are not in the same city or town.

Even though there are other means of communication, such as telephones and the likes, especially in these days of fast electronic media revolution, letters are still a more acceptable way of communicating. Such letters could be sent through e-mails or any other means.

Letters, during this period have several advantages over other means of communication. For instance, it compels you to organize your thoughts logically. Because you have the opportunity of reading it over and again before sending it, you are able to organize your thoughts in a presentable manner.

Secondly, it becomes a document that can be kept, stored and preserved over a period of time for possible future use and references, if need be. This also instills a lot of discipline and caution, especially as it relates to the content and the possibility of a third party seeing it. Whatever you would not want to be reminded of in future, you don't write in such letters.

Thirdly, it comes handy in helping to develop the writer in the art of writing, which may eventually become an asset in future.

This means of communication was very helpful when I was in courtship. We were both in different cities then, and the use of telephones was not as popular. The advantages of communicating through letters listed above are some that we have personally enjoyed. Even now, after so many years, we still make reference to some of those letters. Not too long ago, my husband brought out one of those letters written over twenty years ago, and read some portion of it during a church service. It helped a great deal in driving home some points while he was ministering. What if they were not written in a letter form? It would have been impossible to have them as reference materials!

Enjoying Things Of Mutual Interest

Courtship is not just a time of prayer, fasting, and studying the word of God; although these are of great importance. It is also a time of enjoying things of mutual interest together. For instance, both of you may enjoy taking pictures. Why not? Have fun, but avoid anything sinful. Such pictures can be kept for future references. The other day I saw some pictures that my husband and I took before we got married about twenty seven years ago! It was a lot of fun! Those things help you discover whether you are actually meant for each other or not.

Keep Yourself Pure!

"Flee also youthful lusts: but follow righteousness, faith, charity, peace, with them that call on the Lord out of a pure heart."

2 Timothy 2:22

"Marriage is honourable in all, and the bed undefiled: but whoremongers and adulterers God will judge."

Hebrews 13:4

This word of caution is necessary at this juncture, because when you love an individual and spend time together, there is bound to be a desire to touch, feel, caress and cuddle that person. If care is not taken, one "little" thing will lead to another, until the bed is defiled. I have seen a lot of families in trouble for this reason.

In this part of the world, there is an adage that says that the soup you will eat till night, why must you be in a hurry to steal out of it in the morning? That is as literal as I can get. If you're in courtship, my advice for you is: wait! Be patient. Your time is coming.

If you have been messing yourselves up, defiling the marriage bed, you have to stop it now, so it doesn't stop your destiny. Anyone who defiles the marriage bed is consciously robbing himself/herself of the honour in marriage (Heb. 13:4).

In case you have missed it, if you are genuinely repentant, God will forgive you and restore the honour of marriage back to you; but you must not go back to your vomit, but desist from such acts.

The Next Important Step Towards Marriage

A Formal Engagement

In order to fulfill all righteousness, there is need for a time to formally and publicly introduce yourselves to

83

parents, relations, and friends. In some cultures, it is also a time for the payment of dowry.

Don't just grab a woman and away you go to start living together as man and wife. That is very wrong, especially for a Christian. Wisdom demands that you give honour to the family of your wife/husband-to-be by participating in a formal engagement. Pay the stipulated dowry, but ensure that whatsoever you do, does not violate your Christian principle. Whatever you give as dowry must be things that will glorify God and not condemn your conscience.

I took a closer look at Isaac and Rebekah's wedding. Although it is not a typical wedding, since Isaac did not go in search of Rebekah himself, but we can learn a few lessons from it. In Genesis 24:53, we see that Rebekah's people were only given precious and honourable things, not things for rituals!

> *"And the servant brought forth jewels of silver, and jewels of gold, and raiments, and gave them to Rebekah: he gave also to her brother and to her mother precious things."*

Let me state very clearly here that it is very scriptural to pay dowry! This is a good process to follow.

A U-Turn is Permitted!

Some are in such a hurry to tie the nuptial knot that

they do not take time to get to know each other or refuse to be true to each other. The courtship period is a time to prove all things about your mate. It's true you have decided to spend the rest of your lives together, but you must not take things for granted either. My husband often says humorously that assumption is the mother of frustration! You shall not end your journey in frustration.

"Prove all things; hold fast that which is good."
1 Thessalonians 5:21

If during courtship you discover that two of you cannot "walk" together, that is, you are not compatible and, therefore, cannot make it together, a U-turn is permitted. A U-turn in the sense of putting an end to the courtship. If you feel you have made a wrong choice, call the relationship off! A broken courtship is permitted, if necessary. It is better to break a courtship than to end a marriage in divorce. After all, a broken courtship is not the same as a divorce!

A Public Christian Wedding

Every successful courtship should culminate in marriage. Marriage is a covenant relationship between a man and a woman on the horizontal level, then between God and both of them on a vertical level. For this reason, it is important to have a public Christian

85

wedding ceremony in a Bible-believing church.

When you have your wedding in church, you have formally invited God to be the third party in your union. And Ecclesiastes 4:12 says:

> *"And if one prevail against him, two shall withstand him; and a threefold cord is not quickly broken."*

That is why you must not just pick up a woman, go under a tree, ask your friend to officiate as well as bless the marriage, and that's it! No! Or worst still, both of you just start living together without anything formal. This is one of the reasons many marriages break up after a few years, because a proper Christian wedding is lacking.

It is true that marriage is a covenant relationship between two people, but a public wedding affords members of your family, community, friends and well wishers from far and near the opportunity to share the joy of the day with you.

A public Christian wedding also makes it impossible for people to claim not to know that you are married. Although, in this "fast" age, some young ladies and even men don't mind going out with married men/women, a public wedding helps keep them off! It sanitizes your environment.

What's more? It has been discovered that marriages

conducted in church stands a greater chance of being successful than those that are not.

MAKING WRONG RIGHT

Some people get troubled when they read materials like this, probably because they have been living together with their partners without paying the dowry, having a formal engagement or a public Christian wedding. Rather than feel or live in condemnation, why not make things right? Take steps right away, go and pay the dowry! If you are not legally married and you fall under this category, go and "legalize" your union. This you can do, for instance, by going to the court for a court wedding. Then look for a minister of the gospel to bless your union.

Time never corrects an error! An error yesterday remains an error today, except it is corrected. You can make wrongs right! Many people suffer unduly because they despise this winning path. I have seen women cruelly driven out of their homes at the death of their husbands, because their union was "illegal." The woman has no voice, because she has no legal standing. Wisdom is profitable to direct!

I remember a woman I counselled sometime ago. She had been going through a rough time in her home and was ready to call it quits. To top it up, she had no child. When I interviewed her closely, I discovered a lot of loopholes. Nothing has been given as dowry, and there was nothing legally binding herself and the man together as husband and wife. No court wedding, no church wedding. Both of them just started living together.

I counselled her to ensure that the dowry is paid, legal papers signed in the court of law, and their union blessed by a minister of the gospel. The next time I saw her, she was over-joyed and full of testimonies. To the glory of God, today all is well with that family. To crown it all, she is also expecting a baby!

Parents Beware!

I must sound a note of warning to Christian parents here. Please give room to your children to make their own decisions and accept responsibilities for such. That is the only way for them to grow to maturity. If you do not let them grow, they will groan! Don't insist that they must marry from a particular tribe or someone in a certain profession. As long as the man or woman is of their choice, is born-again, and meets all the other criteria discussed in this chapter, allow them to obey God's leading in their lives concerning marriage. When it is well with them, you also partake of it. It shall be well with you, in Jesus' name!

5

Improve Your Communication Strategy!

In the foregoing chapters, we discussed the family vis-à-vis God's blue print or master plan for it. We have also seen why God wants family success, what constitutes the foundation of a home, and how to go about laying a proper one. But to stop there would be like many building projects terminated mid-way and labeled, "Abandoned Projects". That is why having laid a solid foundation, we need to discuss the various building blocks necessary for the construction of a successful family.

> *"For every house is builded by some man; but he that built all things is God."*
>
> Hebrews 3:4

Building a physical house is hard work! A fantastic

house cannot be wished into existence; it is a product of diligence. Block must strategically come upon block, not to talk of all the other intricacies that go into its construction. A lot of time, money and expertise also come into play.

Families, like a physical house, also require a lot of hard work for it to become glorious. Every member must consciously contribute his/her quota, if it is to succeed. Just as no physical house drops down from the sky, there is no successful family that falls from heaven; rather, any successful family you see was "built".

Prayer is essential to the success of a home, but it is insufficient alone. A couple can kneel down from today till tomorrow praying for a good home. It will all be a wasted effort, except they find out what they need to do to enjoy success and apply themselves to doing it.

A good home takes deliberate efforts to build.

Effective communication is one of the requirements for building a successful marriage and family. The need to constantly improve your communication skills and strategy cannot be over-emphasized.

No matter how effectively you communicate with your spouse and family members right now, you can improve on it. There is always a better way of doing whatever you are doing. Someone has said that the largest room in the world is the room for improvement. Don't ever think that you are communicating the best way possible. You can communicate better than you are right now, if you care to constantly improve the strategies you engage. In this segment, we shall be considering how.

Why Must We Communicate?

The basis for a fruitful and lasting relationship in any family is effective communication. Lack of this is the reason for so much tension in many homes. It can be said to be the "mortar" that cements the marital relationship. Communication is the key to success in marriage. A wise man said, *"If you talk together, you stay together"*, and I believe it is very true. And you know, marriage is about living together!

Let's take a look at the first family, Adam's family; it will help you to appreciate the importance of effective communication. God commanded Adam not to eat of the tree of the knowledge of good and evil. Adam, I suppose, believed, but failed to effectively communicate the seriousness of this command to Eve. She took it lightly, I suppose. If you read the account carefully, you will find that in Eve's dialogue with the serpent, she mentioned that God "said", not "commanded" (Gen. 3:3). But God did not just say it, He commanded it!

"But of the tree of the knowledge of good and evil,
thou shalt not eat of it: for in the day that thou eatest

thereof thou shalt surely die."

Genesis 2:17

The word "commanded" is our point of emphasis. The word actually means "order...authoritative instruction that something be done." A command is non-negotiable and un-debatable. The failure of the first family was the failure of Adam to sit his wife down and make her understand the severity of the issue. (This is not to say that Eve was entirely without fault. If she was not sure what to say to the serpent, she should have asked it to wait until Adam came home!)

The issue is that Adam should have taken the lead in this matter as well. Many families are hitting the rocks today, because the men (husbands) who ought to be taking the lead in matters affecting their families are not! I believe this is one of the strong points in my own family. For example, my husband helped me understand the vision God entrusted into his hands, as well as each new phase it enters into. In turn, I pass down those instructions to our children, so that there's no breakdown in communication at any level.

You must be persuaded of this one thing: marriage is about living lives together; it is a relationship between a man and a woman, who have committed their lives first to God, and then to each other. So, communication must first be one-on-one, between the man and his wife, and then other members of the family. That responsibility cannot be shifted to God. He will not leave heaven to come to your home and speak to your wife or your children on your behalf. It is a non-transferable responsibility!

COMMUNICATING EFFECTIVELY

Many marriages break down as a result of faulty communication. In order to communicate effectively, you need first to understand what communication is, and then the elements that enhance effective communication.

What is Communication?

Defined simply, communication is the art of carrying on a meaningful conversation. It is meant to be two-sided and stimulating. In the home, it is meant to be an avenue of sharing feelings and resolving differences, thereby keeping your relationship on a steady course. The dictionary defines it as "the art of passing information across; the transference of thoughts."

2-Way Conversations

For communication to be effective, it must be two-way. Husband and wife must both participate in conversations, before it can be said to be communication. It is not a conversation if it is one-sided. Open communication cements the marriage relationship and creates a bond that cannot be broken.

Give expression to your life, talk! Some people are not able to reveal their innermost feelings to anyone. This ought not to be in a family relationship. Learn to communicate your feelings, thoughts, joys, fears, challenges, and plans. Discuss them with the one you love!

As you do that, you will discover that the bond between you will grow stronger, and your relationship will be firmly cemented. This will in turn bring unity and mutual respect. Once there is free flow to each other, it becomes a time of sweet fellowship.

It Begins With God

To experience a free flow of communication with your spouse and members of your household, you must develop a good communication with God. That scripture in Hebrews 3:4 helps us understand that although every house is built by some man, He that builds all things is God.

God is the ultimate builder of the family. That is why once a man or woman lacks effective communication with God, communication between family members is affected. Consequently, the quality of your relationship with your spouse will also be affected. Therefore, let the communication lines between you and God be open all the time. Learn to rub minds with Him; as you do,

His great mind will rub off on your little mind, making it sharper.

The question then is, "How do I communicate effectively with God?"

Thanksgiving, Praise and Worship

A life of thanksgiving, praise and worship is the primary way. If you are a "God-praiser", it will reflect in your everyday life with your spouse and family members. You will learn to be appreciative, courteous, considerate and loyal. You will learn to be in harmony with God and people.

> *"...Teaching and admonishing one another in psalms and hymns and spiritual songs, singing with grace in our hearts to the Lord."*
>
> Colossians 3:16

Grace in the heart will automatically produce praise in the mouth! Learn to thank God for what He has done in your life, praise Him for what He is yet to do, and worship Him for who He is! When you do this, you will have nothing to either complain or murmur about. There will then never be a reason to point an accusing finger at God. When you accuse God, who will rescue you?

Accusations, murmuring and complaining are signs of ingratitude. Nothing cripples a conversation like accusations, murmuring and complaining! Flee from it. It is so serious that the Bible says:

"Neither murmur ye, as some of them also murmured, and were destroyed of the destroyer."

1 Corinthians 10:10

"And when the people complained, it displeased the Lord: and the Lord heard it; and his anger was kindled; and the fire of the LORD burnt among them, and consumed them that were in the uttermost parts of the camp."

Numbers 11:1

You think God has not been fair to you, and therefore you complain, murmur and grumble? Remember that God is always right! He is always working in your favour and for your good.

If you know how to talk with God, you will know how to talk with men.

A grateful attitude is the secret!

A Prayerful Life

A life of prayer is another major way of communing with God. Simply defined, prayer is communing with God. It is you talking to God, and God talking to you; it is a two-way purposeful conversation with God.

The apostles asked Jesus in Luke 11:1:

"...Lord, teach us to pray..."

So, prayer has to be taught. Communing with God has to be taught. Philippians 4:6 says:

"Be careful for nothing; but in every thing by prayer and supplication with thanksgiving let your requests be made known unto God."

This clearly shows that through the medium of prayer, your requests can be made known to God, and you can expect answers from Him. What a privilege!

Talking about spiritual gifts in 1 Corinthians 12, the Bible says in verse 2:

"Ye know that ye were Gentiles, carried away unto these dumb idols, even as ye were led."

An idol is a false god. It is something visible, but without substance. One of the characteristics of idols is that they are dumb. But halleluyah, our God is not dumb! God is a talking God! When you talk to God, He talks to you. A talking God communicating with talking men!

Learning how to commune with God greatly improves your communication strategy with men. The starting point for a fruitful conversation with your spouse in particular and family members in general, is a fruitful communion with God. Remember, if you know how to talk with God, you will know how to talk with men.

Two Kinds of Communication

Communication can either be verbal or non-verbal. It is verbal when it involves the use of words. Non-verbal communication involves the use of actions, facial expressions, body language, letters, etc.

Mastering the art of verbal communication is a major secret of success in marriage and family life. Never go to bed at night with something against your wife or husband in your mind. If you do, you may have nightmares and bad dreams! Make sure that whatever needs to be sorted out is done same day. This will go a long way in "cementing" the relationship between you and your spouse, as well as between you and your family members.

When grievances are not aired, an explosion someday is inevitable. It reminds me of what can happen to a bottle of Coca-Cola, when it is shaken repeatedly over a period of time. It will eventually burst open, shattering the bottle. It becomes very important, therefore, for couples and family members to ensure that nothing comes between them that is not sorted out.

"Be ye angry, and sin not: let not the sun go down

upon your wrath: Neither give place to the devil."

Ephesians 4:26-27

When your conversation is meaningful and relevant to your spouse, he will not ignore or shout you down. Never allow any conversation to degenerate into an argument. If you do, you are opening the door to the devil. For many people, winning an argument is more important than winning their spouses. Arguments keep you farther apart from each other, beware of it!

As a woman, for example, you may not agree with a decision made by your husband. The wisest thing to do at that time is to listen to him air his view, and when he has finished, air your own view as well. If for any reason you sense that an argument is about to ensue, suspend the matter till a later date. Communicate your opinion to your Heavenly Father in prayer, and ask for right words, correct timing and approach. But never quarrel!

"He that handleth a matter wisely shall find good: and whoso trusteth in the LORD, happy is he."
Proverbs 16:20

If your conversation always ends in an argument, a gully is being created between both of you; and if not handled on time, it can lead to total separation between you.

It is necessary to mention at this juncture that in a

bid to air their minds, some people speak unadvisedly. This shows lack of discretion. Weigh your words before speaking because words are as fragile as raw eggs; once broken, they cannot be re-gathered.

> *"Let no corrupt communication proceed out of your mouth, but that which is good to the use of edifying, that it may minister grace unto the hearers."*
>
> Ephesians 4:29

Some men call their wives and children all kinds of terrible names, particularly out of anger. Some women in turn are experts at nagging. That is an abuse of the tongue! God did not create the tongue to speak evil words; rather it is meant to be an instrument of edification. Sweet and bitter water cannot proceed from the same source at the same time (Jms 3:11).

Many people misuse their tongue because they lack an understanding of its purpose.

> *"Death and life are in the power of the tongue: and they that love it shall eat the fruit thereof."*
>
> -Proverbs 18:21

> *"Thou art snared with the words of thy mouth, thou art taken with the words of thy mouth."*
>
> -Proverbs 6:2

There are homes that are badly damaged and in serious trouble because the tongue is not being controlled; they are victims of corrupt communication. But Ephesians 4:29 places the responsibility on us. It says,

> **"Let no corrupt communication proceed out of your mouth..."**

You have a responsibility to guard what proceeds out of your mouth.

A woman shared this moving testimony recently:

"Some time in 1990, my husband lost his job and from then, our struggles started. Later, a sister in Christ gave me some money to start a business. Since then, I began to ignore the teachings of the Bishop and his wife on pride, and no longer respected my husband. I insulted him whenever he talked to me, because I was the one fending for the family. He began to complain of the way I talked to him, saying that there was no sign to show that I was born again, that I now was behaving like one of the worldly women.

But yesterday, I came for the International Women Convention, and there was a miming presentation on the use of the tongue. I learnt how to speak correctly to my husband, and regretted the indecent ways I had treated him in the past. On reaching home, I knelt down to greet him and he was surprised, because I had not done that before. There and then, he believed that something good would come out of the convention.

Formerly, whenever he wanted us to have our morning

prayers, I would shun him and tell him to say his own prayers, that I would pray whenever it pleased me. But this morning, I was the one that woke him and the children up for prayers."

— Omotosho, O.

Corrupt communication can rob a couple of marital success. You need to believe God to touch your tongue with coals of fire. No man enjoys a nagging wife. In the same vein, no woman desires a nagging husband. It is time to stop nagging, or it will ultimately stop you.

Another aspect of corrupt communication is gossip. As a family you must guard against gossip. Never be found backbiting and castigating other family members in their absence. It brings hatred and divisions into a home.

Words play a major part in communication. The improvement of communication technology has made our hitherto big world a small place. But many marriages break down as a result of faulty communication. To constantly improve your verbal communication strategy and skills, you must learn how to choose and use right words. Remember, words create atmosphere; so right words will create the right atmosphere, and wrong words, wrong atmosphere. Good relationships are built by right words, which is the vehicle for good communication.

Non-verbal communication involves the use of other

means of conversation other than words. Actions, facial expressions, body language, letters, are all in this category. That reminds me of the popular saying that "Your action speaks so loud, I can't hear your voice"!

You need to understand that of all the things you wear, your expression is the most important. For example, there is a way you can express displeasure without uttering a word. Just by watching your husband's body language, you can tell when he is angry, sad, excited, etc.

The longer you live together with someone, the more you are able to read his or her body language. For example, a look from your husband can send a clear message to you, which no one else may understand. That is non-verbal communication.

In concluding this segment, let me say here that communication is not only vital for husbands and wives, but for all members of the family. Both verbal and non-verbal types of communication are required and should, therefore, be employed by members for a fruitful family relationship. Keep the communication lines open; don't allow the enemy to tamper with it.

Keeping the Communication Lines Open

When you want to have a telephone line connected to your house, the first thing you do is to go to the agency responsible and apply for the same. You are asked to purchase a box to enable you receive and make calls, and then a telephone number is assigned to you.

The moment you are connected, you can freely pick up your receiver and dial any number of your choice, provided you fulfill the required conditions. However, you can only call someone who is also connected! That is not all. The person at the other end must answer the phone call, before any meaningful conversation can take place. In the next few pages, I want to relate this concept to the communication process between husband, wife and members of the family.

Talking and Listening

Communication is a two-way process that involves talking and listening. Husband and wife should make a habit of talking about matters that matter to them. This will involve time, but such time spent is never a waste, but an investment. It is not so much of how long, but how well. Such times help in developing personal relationship with each other, which in turn brings about harmony.

Someone has said, "A good communicator is always a good listener." In essence, a good communicator is not one who talks all the time, but one who knows when to talk and when to listen. There is a time for everything, says the Preacher in Ecclesiastes 3:1.

Can you imagine how frustrating it will be for you to receive a phone call from a friend who spends twenty minutes talking, never allowing you to say a word? You may listen politely the first time, but certainly not the next time. When next he or she calls, you will definitely not be keen to pick up the phone.

For communication to be meaningful, when one person is talking, the other should listen. See what God's word says in James 1:19:

> *"Wherefore, my beloved brethren, let every man be swift to hear, slow to speak, slow to wrath."*

This means that you should listen more than you talk! Someone has said that this is the reason why God gave man two ears, but only one mouth!

One person should not be the only one talking throughout. No matter your temperament, never monopolize a discussion; give room to your spouse or other family members present as well.

If your partner is an introvert, and you are an extrovert, be patient enough to allow him time to talk and wait for him to finish before you respond. This requires discipline, however. Good lovers are usually good listeners! Learn to listen.

The same principle works when you are handling

difficulties or resolving differences. Both of you should speak in turns; one at a time. You should allow your spouse to finish speaking before you talk. Both of you should not be found talking at the same time; before you know it you will be pointing at each other, and the one with larger muscles begins to warm up for a final show down.

God is a God of order, and every thing ought to be done decently and in order!

The Place of Understanding

"Good understanding giveth favour: but the way of transgressors is hard."

Proverbs 13:15

"Through wisdom is an house builded; and by understanding it is established."

Proverbs 24:3

These scriptures reveal the vital place of understanding in establishing a successful family. To establish means to "set up on a permanent basis, to make secure or permanent in a certain place". This means that peace, joy, love, and favour can be set up on a permanent basis in your family. It also means you can secure or make your relationship with your household permanent, by possessing good understanding.

When you possess good understanding, you will correctly interpret what your spouse or family members say, rather than read negative meanings to every statement and action. Understanding helps you read between the lines.

Relating this to the natural, when you receive a call from someone, until you understand what that person is saying, he cannot be said to have communicated. So, it goes beyond talking to understanding, having a clear picture, or what the dictionary defines as to "know and comprehend the nature or meaning of something, realize or grasp (something)". Therefore, understanding is a crucial aspect of communication.

Give Room For Possible Questions

Any seasoned communicator knows that in order to ascertain how effective he has been in passing across a piece of information, he needs a response from his audience. The response can come by way of comments, contributions or questions.

A question is an expression of inquiry that invites or calls for a reply. Relevant questions, when asked, shed light on the subject in question. The reason there is a lot of misunderstanding in some homes (which in most cases results into quarrels), is assumption. Your spouse has said something, you clearly don't understand, and instead of asking for clarification, you assume she means one thing, when actually she means an entirely different thing.

My husband says, "Assumption is the mother of frustration." That means, to assume you understand when you actually did not, invariably leads to frustration. That is one reason so many people are terribly frustrated in their marriage and family life.

Personally, I don't assume I understand a thing. When I am in doubt on an issue, I look for an opportunity to ask relevant questions. There is no crime in asking questions to improve your understanding of a subject matter. If you must not become a question mark, learn to ask questions!

Remember the account between Philip and the Ethiopian eunuch in Acts chapter 8? Read the following verses:

> *"...Understandest thou what thou readest?*
>
> *And he said, how can I, except some man should guide me?...*
>
> *And the eunuch answered Philip, and said, I pray thee, of whom speaketh the prophet this? Of himself, or of some other man?*
>
> *Then Philip opened his mouth, and from the same scripture, and preached unto him Jesus."*
>
> Acts 8:30-35

Asking relevant questions brought complete

transformation for the Ethiopian eunuch, as well as fulfillment of ministry to Philip. Questions are an integral part of communication, if it is going to be meaningful.

As a man, don't just "issue" instructions without giving your wife or children room to ask questions if they have one, or seek clarification. Don't ignore them or shout at them; rather, help their understanding. Spend time to explain until they understand. If Adam had done this, I suppose he would have saved himself and his family a lot of trouble.

The Need For Correct Timing.

In communication, timing is vital. That is, knowing "when" to say "what". Take the example of a woman whose husband is just returning from work, tired. Immediately after welcoming him, she announces to him not to expect any food, because there is nothing in the house. And you wonder why he gets very angry! Remember, "A hungry man is an angry man"!

It may be true that there is no food in the house, but it was said in the wrong way, at the wrong time, and at the wrong place. You must know "when" to say "what". It is foolishness to say things just at any time.

> *"A fool uttereth all his mind: but a wise man keepeth it in till afterwards."*
>
> Proverbs 29:11

The wise still says what is in his heart, but he knows when and where to say it. When there is a matter you want resolved, locate the right place and time. Not when your spouse is hungry or tired, and definitely not in the presence of his or her colleagues.

In presenting an issue, your approach is very important. Also, your approach may be right, but your tone of voice could be demoralizing. Friction in families, in most cases, is as a result of saying the right thing at the wrong time, in the wrong place, or with the wrong voice tone.

> *"A man hath joy by the answer of his mouth: and a word spoken in due season, how good is it!"*
>
> Proverbs 15:23

There is a "due season" for every word! However, it takes wisdom to be able to identify the due season.

In Matthew 25, the Bible talks about the ten virgins who awaited the bridegroom. Five were described as foolish, while the other five were described as wise. I realized that what made the difference between them was timing. Everything the wise ones did, the foolish also did, but at the wrong time. Time is crucial.

The Need For Pure Motives

> *"Now the end of the commandment is charity out*

of a pure heart, and of a good conscience, and of faith unfeigned."

1 Timothy 1:5

God sees beyond what you say to your motive for saying it. Your spouse and family members can hear what you say, but may not know why you said it. That is why the Bible talks about a pure conscience. You must ensure that whatever you are saying is out of a pure conscience

Don't be like some men, who call their wives late at night and say, "Tell me what I said at 10:00 a.m. yesterday? Tell me now. Why are you hesitating? You mean you have forgotten?" And while the wife is trying to re-collect, he slaps her. Don't laugh, it happens! All the man is trying to say is: "I told you not to keep this cup here. Why did you do it?" Instead of a straight forward approach, he chooses rather to make things complicated for her.

God sees your motives for doing what you are doing. Nothing is hid from His all-seeing eyes; not even the thoughts of your heart.

This powerful scripture in Proverbs 15:3 is worthy of note here:

"The eyes of the Lord are in every place, beholding the evil and the good."

This has been my guiding principle in life. It has helped me a great deal in ensuring that my motive for whatever I do, is acceptable to God. My prayer for you is that right from this moment, you will endeavour, by the grace of God, to ensure purity of motive in your communication at all times, especially with your family members.

Gains of Communication

There are gains of effective communication. These include, but are not limited to, the following:

Intimacy. In any home where there is effective communication, **Intimacy** is never lacking. Intimacy here means closeness. This is because the more you learn to communicate, the closer you become; and the closer you are, the more difficult it is for the devil to find access into your relationship. The husband and wife stick together, and therefore stay together.

Friendship is another gain of effective communication. Friendship is based on familiarity and emotional attachment. The more you communicate, the more familiar you become with each other. This in turn gets you attached emotionally to each other. Emotion is part and parcel of love. Emotional attachment is what makes you start feeling for each other. My husband has said that when a husband and wife stop feeling for each other, danger is at the door.

Another gain of effective communication is **self-awareness.** This helps you to know yourself better. Your spouse and family members serve as human mirrors that help you locate the "stains on your back", so a better you can emerge. When the communication lines are open, you are able to better discover yourself through your spouse and/or children. This in turn helps you to discover and correct certain flaws in your life and character, which you may not have known existed before. This subsequently creates acceptance.

One other gain of effective communication is that it **triggers love and submission.** It is a provoker of love from the husband and submission from the wife. Some times, when a woman does not obey the instruction of her husband, it may not necessarily be rebellion or trying to be difficult, but could be because she lacks understanding.

When the communication strategy is constantly improved upon, it stirs up love. When a man communicates well with his wife, it becomes easier to lavish his love on her and the woman in turn finds it is easier to submit to him without being coerced.

If a man finds it difficult to love his wife, it is a sign that he has difficulty communicating with her. But when the communication lines are open, rather than hold grudges, both of them can freely discuss issues and arrive at favourable conclusions.

Personally, I can testify that it is a thing of joy for me to submit to my husband in everything! He doesn't have to coerce me to; I do so willingly and with ease. Not because of his titles, but because the communication lines are open. Effective communication keeps compelling his love in my direction and my submission in his. So then, he confidently looks at me and says: "I just love you."

Children should not be afraid to ask their parents any questions. They should have a sense of being loved, so they don't end up being wayward. Children easily and naturally obey their parents in an atmostphere where the communication lines are open. They understand their parents' instructions so well that disobedience does not thrive in the family.

Because we constantly seek to improve the communication strategy in our home, this helps our children have a good understanding of the vision of God for our family, so they naturally behave in such a way that positively affect the work.

King David, inspite of his busy schedule as king of Israel, created time to communicate effectively with his son, Solomon. He would always extol the virtues of wisdom to him as they communicated.

One of such instances is recorded by Solomon in Proverb 4:3-9. There is a great lesson for all to learn from this, especially fathers.

"For I was my father's son, tender and only beloved in the sight of my mother.

He taught me also, and said unto me, Let thine heart retain my words: keep my commandments, and live.

"Get wisdom, get understanding: forget it not; neither decline from the words of my mouth.

Forsake her not, and she shall preserve thee: love her, and she shall keep thee.

Wisdom is the principal thing; therefore get wisdom: and with all thy getting get understanding.

Exalt her, and she shall promote thee: she shall bring thee to honour, when thou dost embrace her.

She shall give to thine head an ornament of grace: a crown of glory shall she deliver to thee."

No wonder there is this account in 1 Kings 3:5-13:

"In Gibeon the LORD appeared to Solomon in a dream by night: and God said, Ask what I shall give thee.

And Solomon said ... now, O LORD my God, thou hast made thy servant king instead of David my father...Give therefore thy servant an understanding heart to judge thy people, that I may discern between good and bad: for who is able to judge this thy so great a people?

And the speech pleased the Lord, that Solomon had asked this thing.

And God said unto him, Because thou hast asked this thing, and hast not asked for thyself long life; neither hast asked riches for thyself, nor hast asked the life of thine enemies; but hast asked for thyself understanding to discern judgment;

Behold, I have done according to thy words: lo, I have given thee a wise and an understanding heart; so that there was none like thee before thee, neither after thee shall any arise like unto thee.

And I have also given thee that which thou hast not asked, both riches, and honour: so that there shall not be any among the kings like unto thee all thy days."

What a great gain of effective and open lines of communication! Fathers, learn to communicate with your children and teach them the virtues that make for greatness in life. Help them through communication to appreciate the things that are important in life. The reason there are so many thieves and robbers today, is because parents have failed to inculcate good moral values in their children.

Another example is recorded in Proverbs 31:1-5:

"The words of king Lemuel, the prophecy that his

mother taught him.

What, my son? and what, the son of my womb? and what, the son of my vows?

Give not thy strength unto women, nor thy ways to that which destroyeth kings.

It is not for kings, O Lemuel, it is not for kings to drink wine; nor for princes strong drink:

Lest they drink, and forget the law, and pervert the judgment of any of the afflicted."

A child that grows up with this kind of admonition will not wander away from the path of righteousness. So, parents rise up and take your place.

The gains of communication cannot be over emphasized. Open lines of communication between family members can lead to the preservation of lives and destinies. Look at this: it was Abigail's openness that delivered her entire household from the wrath of King David, provoked by the foolishness of Nabal. The communication line was so opened that a steward could approach the "Madam" of the house, to give her valuable information that eventually brought deliverance to her household (I Sam. 25:14).

In conclusion, let me reiterate that constant improvement on your communication strategy is vital for a successful family. You can't do without it!

6

Get Committed!

Commitment is the backbone of any successful relationship, marriage and the family inclusive. It is the adhesive that holds a marriage together. When commitment is lacking in the relationship between a husband and wife, the chances of that family surviving are very slim. What the spinal cord is to the body, is what commitment is to marriage and the family. Without it, the body will be limp and paralyzed.

Families with great success potentials suffer severe set backs and failure, as a result of lack of commitment. I once read the story of a twenty-five year old marriage that ended in separation, due to a lack of commitment of both the husband and wife.

To enjoy family success, you must be committed both to the institution of marriage and to your spouse. Look at this wonderful scripture:

"What therefore God hath joined together, let not man put asunder."

Mark 10:9

Even though God has joined you together, you must be committed to one another, so that nothing is allowed to put you asunder. Again in Genesis 2:24 God's word says:

"Therefore shall a man leave his father and his mother, and shall cleave unto his wife: and they shall be one flesh."

In essence, God is saying that a man shall leave his father and mother and be committed to his wife as well as the institution of marriage and then, by virtue of that commitment, they become one flesh. Same goes for the wife.

Husband, wife, how committed are you to your marriage and family? If you must enjoy family success, then commitment is a must.

What is Commitment?

The Oxford dictionary defines commitment as "an engagement or obligation that restricts freedom of action." In other words, there are some things you cannot do by reason of your commitment. That is why Apostle Paul said in 1 Corinthians 6:12:

"All things are lawful unto me, but all things are not expedient ..."

Commitment makes you choose the expedient above the lawful. It makes you forgo some things that you like or take pleasure in. Sometimes, rights and privileges that are lawfully yours may have to be forfeited in the interest of the family.

Two Levels of Commitment

Commitment is to God and to man (your spouse) . One precedes the other. One is the foundation for the other. A look at Hebrews 3:4 reveals that although every house is built by man, God is the ultimate builder of all things. That means, apart from God, all your building efforts will amount to nothing. John 15:5 reiterates this truth.

"...For without me ye can do nothing."

Commitment to God

Show me a man who is genuinely committed to the Lord, and I will show you one who will be committed to the success of his family. They go hand-in-hand. Any man or woman who is committed to God will without difficulty be committed to his or her spouse.

I remember on September 12, 1976, my husband (then

my fiancé) called me and said, "Are you sure you can marry a man like me?" He wrote a paper he titled "Sailing Under Sealed Orders." I love a particular closing remark he made in that write up. He said, "Christ is either Lord of all or not Lord at all. Where He sends, I will go, what He says, I will do. Even if He asks me to renounce all, I will not even think twice before I do."

Then he asked me to sign, if I was in agreement with the content. I could see his commitment to God and His kingdom and since I was also committed to God, I knew without doubt that we were going in the same direction.

That is why wherever God tells my husband to go today, I don't see myself as having a right to question God or even ask "Why?" I signed up for it many years ago. When we are leaving a city, I don't say, "Oh, what about my friends?" God is greater than anyone else!

Our commitment to God is so deep that I don't feel bad if during a church service my husband whispers in my ears that we are giving an offering of so many millions to God. This is because I signed up for total commitment to God in 1976.

On another occasion, as a nursing mother, I came home with my entire salary, knelt down and presented it to my husband. He said to me, "God spoke to me before you came in that we are to sow everything as a seed." To further complicate the matter, those were the days of scarcity of essential commodities in Nigeria, when they were being rationed. Then, one could have money and not get the commodities to purchase. But with no money at all, what happens? However, the God of all sufficiency was more than enough for us! Instead of being in lack after sowing my entire salary, we became distributors to those around us, by the supernatural supplies of God.

God instituted marriage. The institution of marriage is bigger than the persons in marriage. Therefore, the key to building a successful marriage and family is commitment to the institution of marriage rather, than just to the persons in it.

Marriage is honourable; that is, respectable. The individuals in it sometimes may not be. Marriage, as an institution established by God, is perfect, but the individuals in it are not. People change as they grow, but marriage is constant. It is an unchanging institution. To build a successful marriage, therefore, those in it must learn to honour marriage itself. This is the secret!

Young lady/man, before you agree to marry anyone, find out how committed he/she is to God and to marriage. It is the level of his/her commitment to God that will determine how committed he/she will be to your marriage. Perhaps you married a man who was not committed to God, and now you are wondering why he is not committed to your marriage. He cannot, because the foundation is faulty. He needs to get "sold out" to God first!

However, all hope is not lost. God can give you peace in place of problems, joy where there has been sorrow, and a breakthrough for your breakdowns. He can steady the rocking of your home, just as He calmed the storm in Mark 4:37-39, and their boat stopped rocking.

Give God a chance, by putting to work the things you are reading in this book. Our God is a God of liberation and another chance; He will give you a new beginning, if you let Him!

Commitment to Your Spouse

A successful marriage also requires commitment to your spouse. Without this, no amount of prayer, fasting, and "sleeping" in church can prevent your home from falling apart. Nothing can take the place of commitment in the building of a successful marriage.

Marriage is not a temporary arrangement, but a commitment for life. If this is true, you may wonder why the divorce rate is so high, even among Christians. The reason is that many people are not committed to each other.

Commitment is the framework on which a marriage is

built. A man and his wife must, therefore, be totally committed to each other spiritually, physically, emotionally and otherwise. Commitment in turn brings security.

A successful marriage must be exclusive, involving no other. One man and one woman, in one life-time relationship. Each spouse must commit to "forsake all others".

For example, a woman must be so committed to her husband that no amount of money any other man offers her, to have illicit sex with her, will be strong enough to make her give it a second thought. So also, a man must be so committed to his wife that if his wife and mother were both in a state of emergency and needed rescue, he will naturally rescue his wife first before his mother.

The two levels of commitment we have discussed above can be compared to the hob of a bicycle, which holds all the spokes of the wheel together. However, no matter how effective the spokes may be, without the hob, the bicycle is going nowhere. Therefore, without commitment, no matter what else is in place, that family is going nowhere.

Commitment Compels Love

"Husbands, love your wives, even as Christ also loved the church, and gave himself for it."

Ephesians 5:25

A husband's primary responsibility is that of loving his wife, and commitment compels love. That is, where there is commitment to God and to one's spouse, love becomes automatic. Commitment becomes like a driving force, pushing the husband to love his wife.

When I see a man who finds it difficult to love his wife, I know that the problem is essentially that of lack of commitment to God and to his marriage. When there is commitment, there will be no need to persuade a man to love his wife; it will come naturally.

My husband, for instance, is highly committed to God and to the success of our home, therefore, it is easy for him to ravish me with so much love, even without my asking for it. That is commitment!

Husbands, you need to know this. There is no wife who hates to be loved. There is no woman that will not respond positively to love. Someone once said that submission is a response, because when you love your wife, she responds by submitting. Therefore, tension and quarreling in a home is an indication of the absence of love.

The same principle goes for other members of the family. Commitment to the success of your family makes a man invest time into the lives of his children. He ensures the children have a constant assurance of his love.

Give Voice To Your Commitment

A commitment to love your family is not complete until you give voice to it. Men can never understand what these three simple words, "I love you" can do to a woman. Surprisingly, some men find it difficult to give voice to their commitment.

A man testified during one of our annual conventions that for a long time, he had found it extremely difficult to give voice to his commitment, by expressing his love to his wife. He obeyed the instruction to do so, and things began to change positively in his home.

Expressing love to your legitimate wife or children should not be a difficult thing to do! For some who think it is an unrighteous thing to do, was Jesus unrighteous? Thrice He asked Peter if he loved Him. Remember that Jesus was never married, but His disciples represented His earthly wife in a figure. So in essence, He was saying to His "wife", "I love you; do you love Me?"

Don't read this book without putting the contents to work. Husbands, if you have not been giving voice to your commitment, it is time to get started. And if you already have, there is still room for improvement. Learn to look straight into her eyes and tell her how much you love her and you will see the change in her countenance.

No matter how spiritual a woman is, she still wants

to be told that she is loved. I can tell you this, as a woman I want to hear my husband give voice to his commitment, by telling me how much he loves me, and he does! These are some of the things that hold our home together.

I must say a word concerning children here. Children like to be touched and cuddled. A touch communicates warmth. Hug them, kiss them; let them feel a sense of being connected with you, by your warm embraces. It is not unrighteous. It is a mortar bonding you together. It keeps the assurance of your love burning at times when words are clumsy.

Commitment Triggers Submission

Just as commitment provokes love, it also triggers submission. Any woman who is truly committed to the success of her marriage will be submissive to her husband. When a woman is stubborn and naughty, it is a sign of lack of commitment to her home.

What is submission? Simply defined, it means willingly putting yourself under someone else's authority. Contrary to some people's thinking, submission has nothing to do with slavery. Rather, it is an act of the will. A committed woman needs no advice to submit to her husband. Her commitment is a driving force. I am not talking about submission under duress, but from a willing heart.

Many people wish and express their desire that their home be like ours, but as the saying goes, "If wishes were horses beggars will ride." Nothing good happens by chance. Commitment must be in place, else family success will be a mere dream.

Thank God for His grace, but we have been committed to playing our parts too. That is why today, I can boldly declare that I am enjoying a good home! As you play your part also, God will give you a brighter testimony than ours!

Wherever there is commitment in a marriage, there will be love and submission: both parties working together for the success of their home.

Personally, I don't find it stressful to submit to my husband. Not just now, but right from the days of little beginnings. I never had to be coerced into doing so. I always have found it a thing of great joy.

Single ladies, before you get into a marriage relationship with any man, ensure that you can submit to him without duress. If you find it difficult to submit to him during courtship, then don't marry him! This is because you will not submit to him in marriage, and that is signing in for trouble.

An area where many women find it difficult to submit in marriage is in their finances. Money is a "god" to such women. They may submit to the man in other areas, but when it comes to finances, forget it! I learnt to submit my earnings to my husband right from the time I was engaged in secular employment. Mark you, I was not just throwing it at him, but handing it over to him respectfully. That's why now he does not wait for me to ask for money; he just keeps giving to me!

I would, however, like to sound a note of caution here, for the sake of balance. It was easy for me to hand over my salary to my husband because our relationship permitted that. I could trust him. He was not bullying me or spending the money in an unaccountable manner. Men, if you want to enjoy this type of co-operation from your wife, make sure you build a relationship with her that will permit that. Don't expect your wife to hand over her earnings to you if you treat her with disrespect, or if you are uncommunicative and unaccountable in your spending habits. Don't expect her to submit all her income to you if you are going to spend it frivolously, without any consideration for her own needs as well.

Woman, don't hand over all your income to a husband who is not responsible for the family upkeep, children's school fees, household bills, etc. or who spends all the money on riotous living – drinking, womanizing, etc. Wisdom is profitable to direct (Eccl.10:10). Your attitude must, however, remain humble and non-confrontational.

Commitment on the woman's part also demands that she respects her husband. I am yet to find a man who hates to be respected! Lack of respect for the husband is what makes some men engage in physical combat with their wives (although this is not to justify such action). How some women address their husbands show they lack an understanding of family government as ordained by God.

Woman, respect is reciprocal; it's give and take. If you give respect, you will earn respect. For instance, some wives are too "modern" to greet their husbands. He wakes up in the morning, and she's staring at him; no word of greetings. But she greets everyone else outside, with a smile for that matter. First get committed to the success of your marriage, and then you will get God committed.

Commitment is in Three Realms

Man is a spirit, possessing a soul and lives in a body. In other words, man is tripartite. If that is true, and it is, it means that God expects commitment in marriage to affect the three realms – spirit, soul and body. Understanding this is crucial to the success of any union.

Spiritually, be committed to the spiritual demands of your family. Husbands, you are the high priest and prophet of the family. You are to take the lead in the spiritual well-being of the family. Take time out to pray for the family, even fasting sometimes when the need arises. Lead the family by your example of commitment and devotion to God and the cause of the kingdom. Spend time with the family in prayer and studying of the Word of God.

Wives, you are the family's spiritual anchor. You are created to be very perceptive and therefore, you are able to sense things when no other person can. At times like that, be committed to taking such issues to God in prayer. The story of the mother of the Wesleys cannot be over-emphasized. It is on record that she took every child daily in prayers, communication and quality relationship. It was, therefore, impossible for her children to miss their places in destiny. Her commitment to her family has paid off for posterity.

Mentally also, a husband and wife should be committed to the mental development of their family. Show the children the right way to mental excellence. Invest in their mental development by buying them books and other educational materials that will enhance their mental dignity. Please do not buy things that will corrupt their minds, all in the name of flowing with the trend.

Physically, the family welfare must be given the utmost priority that it requires, if family success must be realised. You cannot expect your family to be successful if you deprive them of the basic necessities of life. So, do your best to ensure your family enjoys the best you can provide. You will make it, in Jesus' name!

Can You Be Trusted?

Trust is an essential, vital ingredient in our daily family walk. No family can experience true success without it. Someone has defined trust as communication + commitment + time. Trust thrives in an atmosphere of effective communication and commitment. There is trust in a family where there is communication and commitment that has passed the test of time. Trust takes time and effort. It is easily broken and hard to restore; but if you are willing to put to work what it takes to make it work, the reward is the successful family you have always dreamt of.

What is Trust?

The Oxfords dictionary defines trust as the firm belief in the reliability, truth or strength of a person; confident expectation, obligation or responsibility; the state of being relied upon. That is why the Psalmist said of the

Lord in Psalms 18:2:

> *"The LORD is my rock, and my fortress, and my deliverer; my God, my strength, in whom I will trust; my buckler, and the horn of my salvation, and my high tower."*

In a practical sense, trust means that you place confidence in someone to be honest with and faithful to you, and not abandon you. You cannot touch, taste, see, smell or hear trust; yet, no successful family or anyone desiring one, can live a day without its effect. Trust is part of our daily life. Each time we flip a switch, sit on a chair or turn the doorknob, we trust that something we expect will happen. Often, we do not even need to pray or fast before we take these actions. Why? We have over time come to realise that these things respond naturally to our touch.

Trust is not a gift. It is a virtue built through experience and over a period of time. Trust is reciprocal. The more you express your trust to members of your household, the more they respond to you in trust. You can also rebuild trust in broken relationships, when you make a choice to do so, with the supernatural help of God. Trust grows over time. Building trust takes time, and you need to show your partner that you are trustworthy and that you trust them in return.

"As for God, his way is perfect: the word of the

LORD is tried: he is a buckler to all those that trust in him."

Psalms 18:30

Even God's Word is tried first before trust in it can be developed, and this takes time. The same goes for building a successful family. Your family relationship must come to a point where every one responds to the other truthfully. You cannot have a successful family if each time, one member of the family says or does a thing, you are second-guessing their real intent and rephrasing their statements and/ or actions, to fit into your own agenda.

Why Trust?

The very essence of life depends on trust. You go to bed at night with a perfect plan for the next day, because you trust you will wake up the next morning. You eat your food confident that your body network is designed to digest the food. You go to work everyday, trusting that the job you closed from yesterday, is still there waiting for you. You breathe freely without bothering to crosscheck the oxygen level or quality of the air. All these actions are performed without concern, because of trust.

No successful family relationship can survive an environment devoid of trust between members. A married couple must learn to trust each other. If your marriage must work, you need to be able to trust your spouse with your past, present and future. Marriage is dependent on the confident belief that you are loved and accepted the way you are. The knowledge of the fact that you are loved the way you are, helps you relax and let down your guard. It makes room for honesty without fear of rejection, and that feels good. One of the virtues of the virtuous woman aptly painted in Proverbs 31:11 is this:

"The heart of her husband doth safely trust in her, so that he shall have no need of spoil."

He is confident that his wife can be trusted to take care of certain issues that affect the family. That was why some years ago, my husband came to my office and handed me a blank cheque booklet, all signed. He had found me trustworthy in the handling of financial matters, and therefore, could trust me with the handling of the money in that account without regretting such action.

Children born in a home where there is an open display of trust, grow up more emotionally balanced than those bred in an atmosphere of dishonesty. They are more confident in life and approach issues with a right sense of judgment. The reason we have many children in all manner of vices today, is because the vital key of trust is missing. They do not feel their parents' trust, and so really care less if any other person wants to trust them. They develop a rebellious spirit and are very self-defensive, even when there is no need for it.

How To Build Trust

If trust is this important, then how do you build it? Trust does not naturally happen between two people or members of a family, even though they love each other. It takes work and a commitment to build. Your past experiences sometimes may affect your ability to trust. If you had been hurt in the past, it can be especially difficult. The good news, however, is that in Christ there is hope, for:

"...All things are by the law purged with blood ..."

Hebrews 9:22

The blood of Jesus was shed to cleanse us of all forms of unrighteousness, which includes all our past hurts and disappointments. If we will let God, He will eliminate all our past and give us the grace, strength and courage to build trust once again. Remember, we are all growing into perfection. So, be quick to forgive your spouse or other members of your household, when there has been a disappointment of expectations.

In building trust, you need to be truthful. Be truthful to your spouse and family members. Don't be found to say one thing today and another tomorrow on the same issue. There is no substitute for truth! Your yea must be found to be yea, and your nay found to be nay. If you are a person with double standards, it becomes difficult to trust you.

Even with your children, always say what you mean. The home becomes an untrustworthy environment, when people make threats or say things they don't mean. They become empty words. So all the, "I will beat you" threats you issue to your children that have become a play sentence, will only destroy their level of trust in your words and person. It is very important that members of your household can trust what you say.

It is only men of truth that are considered for positions of responsibility.

"Moreover thou shalt provide out of all the people able men, such as fear God, men of truth, hating covetousness; and place such over them, to be rulers of thousands, and rulers of hundreds, rulers of fifties, and rulers of tens."

Exodus 18:21

Effective rulership of your family can only be established, when members of the household know your commitment to truth. Truth commands and compels respect.

Truth is a defense. Your integrity will speak for you

in the day of adversity. It was what happened with Hezekiah when he was to die before he fulfilled the number of his days. He cried to God thus:

"... O LORD, remember now how I have walked before thee in truth and with a perfect heart, and have done that which is good in thy sight..."

-2 Kings 20:3

God had to send Isaiah back to him, to inform him of the extension of his life by another fifteen years. The level of your boldness with your children, will be greatly enhanced when they can trust you with the truth at all times.

Another way to build trust is by keeping your promises to your family members. Promises have a way of creating excitement. It brings anticipation and hope, and if not kept, destroys trust. If for any reason you are not able to keep one, ensure that a thorough and honest explanation is given for it. Particularly in child raising, hope and trust in God and the society can be built or destroyed by our level of commitment to the fulfillment of our promises to our children. Don't make promises you know you will not fulfill, just to get your children off your back. Children find it very difficult to understand why a parent will promise to do something and fail to do so. Learn to follow the example that God has left for us.

"Blessed be the Lord, that hath given rest unto his people Israel, according to all that he promised: there hath not failed one word of all his good promise, which he promised by the hand of Moses his servant."

1 Kings 8:56

"They looked unto him, and were lightened: and their faces were not ashamed."

Psalms 34:5

You will not know shame in your family, in Jesus' name!

It is very important that spouses in a marriage respect, appreciate, and fulfill their marriage vows to each other. That is the only way to build trust. Remember that trust is built over a period of time. It is in the keeping of your vows to one another that trust is built. Trust cannot thrive in a home where there is no respect or regard for each other and the vows of marriage binding you to each other. When you deal treacherously with your spouse, even God is offended (Mal. 2:14).

Also, building trust demands that you be loyal to your spouse, especially in his/her absence. Loyalty breeds trustworthiness. The word loyal is defined by the American Heritage Dictionary to mean "steadfast in allegiance to one's home... faithful to a person, ideal, custom, cause, or duty." Loyalty means a "feeling or attitude of devoted attachment and affection. It means faithfulness to a person or a cause."

In other words, loyalty demands that your allegiance to your spouse and family must be in place, in order for you to build a successful family. Don't betray any of your family members. Betrayal destroys trust. For instance, as a mother, when your children trust you with some information, it is not for you to make it the subject of your dinner time conversation. A child in that situation will find it very difficult to entrust you with any other information he/she considers private and confidential.

True friendship is also negatively affected when there is a betrayal of trust. Believe in each other, and tell each other the truth at all times.

In building a successful family, there must be confident expectations that weaknesses or confidences will not be betrayed. The story of Isaac and Rebekah in Genesis 27 shows us clearly the harmful effect of the destruction of trust between couples. Rebekah engineered Jacob to deceive Isaac, using the weakness of his sight to obtain his father's blessings. It is interesting to note that that was the last effective contribution Rebekah ever made to life. That is a great lesson to learn. Your light will not be put out in obscurity!

Talking about the loyalty of Jesus, a writer said: "When we look at Jesus, we see that He did not live with a sense of open options. He was steadfast in His allegiance to the will of His father in heaven. He was faithful to His twelve disciples, bearing with them through thick and thin. Long after you and I would have given up on them, He was loyal to them."

Loyalty demands that whatever you can't say in the presence of a family member, you should not be found saying it in his/ her absence. In the same vein, what you will be ashamed to be identified with, don't say either in his/ her presence or absence.

Another very vital key needed for the building of trust in a family is forgiveness. Forgiveness in a marriage and among family members is not just an admonition, but a commandment. It is so vital that no marriage or family can survive its absence. As members of a family, you must learn the act of forgiving one another.

Phillip Yancey wrote: "Forgiveness is another way of admitting, 'I'm human, I make mistakes, I want to be granted that privilege, and so I grant you that privilege". "None of us is without sin. The Bible says in Romans 3:23-24:

> *"For all have sinned and fall short of the glory of God; Being justified freely by his grace through the redemption that is in Christ Jesus."*

You are not always right yourself; you are only right in your own eyes. The Psalmist realising this, in Psalms

19:13 prayed earnestly to be delivered from presumptuous sins. You are only a product of grace. That is why the Bible says:

> *"Every way of a man is right in his own eyes: but the Lord pondereth the hearts."*
>
> Proverbs 21:2

> *"The way of a fool is right in his own eyes: but he that hearkeneth unto counsel is wise."*
>
> Proverbs 12:15

If God were to consider your own misdemeanors, where would you stand?

> *"If thou, Lord, shouldest mark iniquities, O Lord, who shall stand?*
>
> Psalms 130:3

Since we are to be like Christ, then our forgiveness should be based on a new standard: one that grants forgiveness unconditionally, without the requirement of payment or the promise of change. Jesus, hanging from the cross in Luke 23:34, looked at the same people who had crucified Him and could still say:

> *"Father, forgive them; for they know not what they do."*

And to the thief on the cross, who by simple expression

of faith in Him, in Luke 23:43, He said:

" ... Today you shalt be with me in paradise."

That's unconditional forgiveness! There was no time for the thief to change first, before he could enjoy the forgiveness he needed to get into heaven. Jesus declared forgiveness and reconciliation without any conditions to be met.

This is the right approach to forgiveness, in building trust in a marriage and among family members. It is the dimension of forgiveness my husband refers to humourously as "advance forgiveness." Seek to know and experience Christ's love and forgiveness in your own life, and that will make it easy for you to make a choice to forgive others.

In building a successful family, all issues that have caused hurts, bitterness and resentments must be resolved daily before you go to bed, so you can rise up in the morning on a fresh note. The Bible says:

"Be ye angry, and sin not: let not the sun go down upon your wrath."

Ephesians 4:26

"Looking diligently lest any man fail of the grace of God; lest any root of bitterness springing up trouble you, and thereby many be defiled."

Hebrews 12:15

Bitterness embitters destiny, flee from it! Many people are well dressed, but rotten within, because of bitterness. Unforgiveness is the root of bitterness, and it destroys. Forgiveness is its medicine! It is the wisdom of God.

Lastly in building trust, you must be accountable. Accountability is defined as "responsible: responsible to somebody else or to others, or responsible for something." Each member of the family must be conscious of the fact that they owe other members accountability in the handling of the affairs of the family, bearing in mind that even God will demand accountability from us.

> *"So then every one of us shall give account of himself to God."*
>
> Romans 14:12

Whatever your placement in the family, whether as father, mother or children, there are things for which God will hold you personally responsible. Like I said earlier in this book, there is a purpose for which God made you a member of that family. He expects you to fulfill that purpose, and will hold you accountable for the non-performance of that task.

Accountability begins with the readiness to be held accountable for your actions. One major challenge of building a successful family is the vice of self-justification. No one wants to accept responsibility for anything that has gone wrong. There is always someone else to blame for our actions or inactions. The graphic picture painted in the Garden of Eden is very illustrative of this point:

> *"And the LORD God called unto Adam, and said unto him, Where art thou?*
>
> *And he said, I heard thy voice in the garden, and I was afraid, because I was naked; and I hid myself.*
>
> *And he said, Who told thee that thou wast naked? Hast thou eaten of the tree, whereof I commanded thee that thou shouldest not eat?*
>
> *And the man said, The woman whom thou gavest to be with me, she gave me of the tree, and I did eat.*
>
> *And the LORD God said unto the woman, What is this that thou hast done? And the woman said, The serpent beguiled me, and I did eat."*
>
> Genesis 3:9-13

That is the nature of the fallen man. Perhaps the path to redemption would have taken a different cause had Adam simply accepted responsibility for his action and sought forgiveness. God is plenteous in mercy; just maybe Jesus would not have needed to pay the ultimate price of death, to reconcile us back to God. Sometimes, some families have had to go through hard times and in some cases, suffer some irreparable losses, just because one of the members refused to accept responsibility.

Responsibility is a sign of maturity. Until you are matured enough to be accountable for rights and wrongs done, you cannot be said to be responsible enough to handle the affairs of life. Life itself is a product of personal responsibility. I am appalled when I find or counsel people who blame their kith and kin or the society or economy for their failures. Life will only answer to you, when you are ready to accept responsibility for what it will take to make it work. The same is true of building a successful family.

Trust in a family can only be built when each member, particularly the parents, are matured enough to take the lead in accepting responsibility for making the family a place of honour and dignity. Children who grow up in a home where the parents are ready to accept responsibility and where there is an open expression of apology for all irresponsible acts, tend to also live responsible lives. In raising your children, one of the virtues they should find in you is accountability. The goal for accountability is for us to grow strong and take responsibility for our lives. The focus must be growth, not just preservation.

Accountability is always mutual. Parents must realise that they are accountable to their children too. When you give account to members of your family, they also feel compelled to be accountable. Trust, respect, honour, love and submission grow as we become more accountable.

The goals, objectives, strategies, and means for communicating accountability must be made clear for it to be effective. Every member of the family must understand the need to be accountable one to another. For instance, a man must realise that trust is built when he lets members of his family know his whereabouts at all times, even if it is around the neighbourhood. He should not just run into a friend on the way and decide to follow him home without first telling someone in his household his whereabouts. The same goes for every member of the household. All forms of suspicions are eliminated in a family setup this way. In this wild and evil world we live in today, accidents or losses can be avoided this way. Several people have lost their lives to such careless and unaccountable movements. Even their family members could not trace their corpses, because they had no idea where to look. Sometimes, people are not even sure whether the person is dead or still alive.

Clear lines of accountability should be well defined to all members of the family. Every member of the family must also be made to realise the specific responsibilities for which they will be held accountable. For instance, it should be clearly understood by all that the father is the head of the family union. The mother is known to be the manager of the family affairs, and the children also have certain responsibilities to fulfill such as household chores, a commitment to school or work, whichever applies at their level, and so on. This type of clarity allows trust to be built and prevents self-justification.

Sometimes, there is a breakdown of accountability when family members are assigned responsibilities and the needed authority to make it work is not provided. Every member of the family, particularly the parent in the home, must effectively stand in their positions of authority in the home government to ensure accountability. Time and avenues should also be provided for everyone to give an account of the responsibilities given to them per time. It is only human to take seriously a responsibility for which you know you will be checked. Not everyone is good at working without supervision.

In building a successful family, therefore, the aim of accountability is to teach every member of the family to take personal responsibility for their actions and be conscious of the subsequent effect of these actions on the entire family.

Benefits of Trust

Trust is fundamental in building a successful family, because it creates an environment for intimacy to grow between family members. True and lasting intimacy can only be built with trust as its backbone. Just as building trust takes time, so does intimacy; it does not grow naturally, and it is not something that can be enforced. Intimacy will only thrive where everyone feels a sense of safety and confident trust in the integrity of the other members involved.

Intimacy is defined as "a feeling of being intimate and belonging together; close in friendship or acquaintance." What trust does in a family is to bring all the members of the family closer together, with a sense of true belonging one to another in an atmosphere of true friendship.

A family that enjoys intimacy must of a necessity command the blessings of the Lord. For:

> *"Behold, how good and how pleasant it is for brethren to dwell together in unity...for there the LORD commanded the blessing, even life for evermore."*

Psalms 133: 1, 3

Children brought up in an atmosphere of true intimacy are usually very emotionally balanced. They find it easier to resist and overcome peer pressures, because they feel so much love and affection from their family members such that no void exist that is yearning for satisfaction. Intimacy involves both physical and emotional interaction. Emotional intimacy helps to breed an open sharing of feelings, experiences and thoughts in a very honest way among family members.

Secondly, trust eliminates fear.

> *"Behold, God is my salvation; I will trust, and not be afraid: for the LORD JEHOVAH is my strength and my song; he also is become my salvation."*
>
> Isaiah 12:2

Perhaps one of the greatest benefits of trust in building a successful family is the elimination of fear. Fear is a spirit, which gives birth to jealousy and insecurity in a family setup. These are destroyers of peace in the family.

Fear is defined as "a feeling of agitation and anxiety caused by the presence or imminence of danger." Sometimes the feeling of insecurity among family members leads to an unwarranted apprehension of marital unfaithfulness. Trust helps to eliminate this. Trust is also defined as "firm reliance on the integrity, ability, or character of a person or thing." When the integrity of members of a family can be attested to, then the spirit of fear is completely eliminated in the family setup.

With the elimination of fear in any family comes strength. Confidence in the integrity and character of members of a family releases the strength to work together to make things work. The force of unity in the home becomes the secret of their Christian testimony.

> *"The LORD is my rock, and my fortress, and my deliverer; my God, my strength, in whom I will trust; my buckler, and the horn of my salvation, and my high tower."*
>
> Psalm 18:2

In conclusion, please note that trust takes time and patience to build. It is not a gift; it is a virtue that requires a conscious, deliberate effort to build; and it begins with you.

Dwell According To Knowledge

The major reason for crises in families today, is because family members do not fully understand, their God-given responsibilities in the family set up. A person cannot do that which he does not know. If a person does not know his duties in the family setup, he cannot fulfill his obligations. In this chapter, I shall be examining one of the vital responsibilities necessary for achieving family success.

In 1 Peter 3:7 the Bible records:

> *"Likewise, ye husbands, dwell with them according to knowledge, giving honour unto the wife, as unto the weaker vessel, and as being heirs together of the grace of life; that your prayers be not hindered."*

The main emphasis here is the phrase, "Dwell with them according to knowledge." The word "dwell" is translated from the Greek word "sunoikeo", which is used to denote domestic association and this association is to be done according to knowledge. For any family to experience any degree of success, a knowledge of the nature and duties of every member of the family is inevitable. What then is knowledge?

The Oxford dictionary defines "knowledge" as awareness or familiarity gained by experience of a person. Dictionary.com defines it as "the state or fact of knowing; familiarity, awareness, or understanding gained through experience or study; specific information about something."

When the Bible, therefore, enjoins us to dwell according to knowledge, it means there are certain facts that one must lay hold on in order to enjoy family success. There are lots of family crises when we have little or no knowledge of our duties in fulfilling God's ultimate purpose for the family. That is why the Bible says in Hosea 4:6:

"My people are destroyed for lack of knowledge..."

Each member of the family has a certain God-given responsibility to fulfill in the family, in order for success to abound therein. My husband has often shared one of the secrets of our family success, which is the acquisition of knowledge. By reason of what he saw of the marriage institution in his growing up days, he began seeking to know from God, His true purpose for the institution of marriage. It was in that state that God showed him the seven concepts of marriage, which has been practiced conscientiously in our family, causing us to enjoy a great deal of success. It took knowledge for us to know our individual placement in the family network, and that knowledge has set us free from every family crises.

To enjoy family success, therefore, the place of knowledge cannot be over emphasized. In Proverbs 24:3-4 the NIV Bible, enumerating the benefits of knowledge, says:

"By wisdom a house is built, and through understanding it is established; through knowledge its rooms are filled with rare and beautiful treasures."

If you must find rooms (families) which are filled with rare and beautiful treasures of peace, love, joy, satisfaction, sunshine, fulfillment, etc, then knowledge is the key. It takes knowledge to enjoy family success.

The prescription to dwell according to knowledge within the family network has its source in God. Therefore, I will be looking at His instruction on the subject, for the Bible has said in Proverbs 2:6

"For the LORD giveth wisdom: out of his mouth cometh knowledge and understanding."

The scriptures often use the words wisdom, knowledge

and understanding interchangeably. But they are occasionally spoken of as separate and distinct. Knowledge is the facts, understanding is the ability to lift the meaning out of the facts, and wisdom is knowing what next to do.

Knowledge is the ability to collate and access information. This alone may not be beneficial, except the information gathered is understood, leading you to the next line of action. Understanding, on the other hand, is the ability to extract meaning out of information, which produces principles; while wisdom is the ability to decipher which principles to apply now.

The injunction to dwell according to knowledge will not be beneficial without an understanding of what one's responsibilities are, and a decision to put them to work. This chapter is dedicated, therefore, to the biblical instructions to husbands, wives and children concerning their covenant responsibilities, blessings, and privileges.

Duties of The Men

To the husbands we read in the Bible:

"Husbands, love your wives, and be not bitter against them."

Colossians 3:19

"Likewise, ye husbands, dwell with them according

to knowledge, giving honour unto the wife, as unto the weaker vessel, and as being heirs together of the grace of life; that your prayers be not hindered."

1 Peter 3:7

"Husbands, love your wives, even as Christ also loved the church, and gave himself for it.

So ought men to love their wives as their own bodies. He that loveth his wife loveth himself.

For no man ever yet hated his own flesh; but nourisheth and cherisheth it, even as the Lord the church."

Ephesians 5:25, 28-29

A man's primary responsibility in the family is to care for and generally oversee the welfare of his family. A great burden is placed on the man to love his wife as Christ loves the Church, and he is not exempted from this responsibility even if his wife is not submissive or is unsaved. This responsibility can be accomplished only through sacrifices, being a godly example, and through an unconditional devotion, commitment and dedication to his family.

Your wife is your chief concern, second only to God. Matthew 5:43-48 defines this type of love beautifully. There Jesus enjoined us that human love must be patterned after the manner of God's love. God sends His rain on both the just and unjust, and makes His sun to shine on the good and the bad. This kind of love is generous and with an unconditional goodwill. It will never seek anything but the highest good of the family. Likewise, irrespective of the behaviour of other members of the family, the man must always seek their highest good.

The man is the head of the household and bears the responsibility for the entire family unit. His leadership position as head of the union places a great responsibility on him to protect, care for, and seek the general well-being of his family: spiritually, physically, and emotionally. This kind of love must be seen in action, and not in mere words. A man can tell members of his family all day long that he loves them, but until he shows them that love, his words will do little to strengthen their family relationship. This dimension of love also demands that even if they treat him wrong, he must treat them right every time.

The husband should encourage the spiritual development of his family, as Christ encouraged the spiritual development of His disciples. He must even be prepared to lay down his life for them, if necessary. This includes giving up selfish hobbies and past times which take him away from the family unit or drain needed resources from the family budget. For the spiritual development of the family, it is also required that the husband leads his household in the study of God's word and in regular family devotions. He is to take the lead, particularly by example, in the worship of God. In addition, a man cannot direct the affairs of his family without first having daily fellowship with the Lord in prayers and the study of the Bible.

Also included in the meaning of "dwell with them according to knowledge" is the intimate knowledge of your wife and family members. Familiarity breeds intimacy. The man must take the time and make the effort to know what his wife and family members like and dislike, what makes them happy and sad, and what makes them secure and insecure, and strive to satisfy or please them. A man is to be sympathetic to the desires and feelings of his household. He must also always consider their physical and emotional needs.

A man of wisdom said, and I agree with him, that the more we know God, the greater love for God we will have, and the greater allegiance and obedience we will yield to Him. The same is true of the family. The more a man knows his family and his responsibilities towards them, the more he will love his family and desire to serve and provide for them. The only way to acquire the required knowledge in all these areas, is by a diligent study of God's Word (2 Tim.2:15).

Another fundamental duty of the man is to honour

his wife and other members of the family. This perhaps is an even higher level of responsibility than just providing for their physical needs. Respect, they say, is reciprocal. If a man must enjoy respect from members of his household, then he must be willing first to invest in it. He must respect, admire, appreciate, praise and exalt his family. These he does by his chaste conduct, behaviour and speech. A man who is soft spoken to members of his family, will most certainly reap a chaste conversation from his household. A harsh-tongued man will definitely raise a family with harsh and nagging tongues.

A man should not be a tyrant. A man and his wife are equal before God, though they have different functions. Husbands and wives are to submit to one another (Col. 3:18, 1Pet. 3:1-7). It should be noted that women are not inferior, nor are they subservient in status to the men. Though a woman is equal to her husband, yet by the marriage covenant she has chosen to submit herself to her own husband (Gen. 24:8,58), even though she is equal in status to other men. If a man, therefore, recognises this important fact, it becomes easy for him to give honour to his wife.

Duties Of The Women

To the wives we read:

"Wives, submit yourselves unto your own husbands, as it is fit in the Lord."

Colossians 3:18

"That they may teach the young women to be sober, to love their husbands, to love their children,

To be discreet, chaste, keepers at home, good, obedient to their own husbands, that the word of God be not blasphemed."

Titus 2:4-5

"Wives, submit yourselves unto your own husbands, as unto the Lord.

For the husband is the head of the wife, even as Christ is the head of the church: and he is the saviour of the body.

Therefore as the church is subject unto Christ, so let the wives be to their own husbands in every thing."

Ephesians 5:22-24

The woman's primary responsibility, after the Lord, is to her husband and children. The woman received the title of "help meet" in Genesis 2, which clearly established her role in the family, as one of a support to her husband. The Bible specifically demands of the woman submission in all things.

A man of wisdom, David Lipscomb, wrote, "The submission of the wife to the husband is that of love, respect and reverence, which is befitting the relation she holds to her husband. In her sphere, she is spiritually on an equality with man, but as a husband, he is the natural scripturally recognised head and leader of the family. Her submission must be in accordance with the principles of righteousness, and nothing is required of her inconsistent with Christian character."

In dwelling according to knowledge, a woman must recognise and put to use the knowledge of her placement in the family, in order to enjoy a successful family. The idea of submission is a stumbling block to many women, because they equate submission with inferiority. Men and women are created co-equal by God, but for the purpose of His plan of redemption, God has assigned to each of them differing roles to carry out. God has clearly called the wife to submit to her own husband. That is God's design ordained for her blessings.

The matter of submission is very clearly indicated in the verses quoted above. The wife is to submit to her husband. The manner of submission is as unto the Lord, and the motive is God's design to make the husband the head of the wife. The model is the way the Church submits to Christ, and the extent is in everything. That is God's design for the woman in the family setup.

A man of wisdom once said, "When purpose is not known, abuse is inevitable." The reason women find it difficult to be submissive is because they do not know the motive for submission and the manner in which submission is to be rendered. Ephesians 5:23 clearly points out the motive for submission:

"For the husband is the head of the wife."

That's God's design, that's the divine plan.

Just as a body submits to the brain located in the head by design, so the wife should submit to the husband, who is the head. When you see a body that does not respond to the head, you see a deformity, you see something that is not normal. You see a dysfunctional person. The same is true in a marriage. Where a wife does not submit to her husband, there is distortion, deformity, and dysfunction. God has designed that the body respond to the head, and the husband is the head of the wife.

In the same verse 23, we see the model of submission: *"As Christ is the head of the church."* In other words, a woman is to submit to her husband as the Church submits to Christ. With the same complete, non-grudging, joyful and willing heart that the Church has in obeying Christ, the wife is to submit to her husband, in order for the woman to enjoy success in her family.

Women should seek the Lord diligently and strive to be chaste in conduct, behaviour, and dressing. The woman has the duty to pursue opportunities to serve in appropriate capacities and pursue those skills necessary for homemaking (Prov. 31:10-30). Sarah was found pleasing to the Lord because of her submission to Abraham, and as a result, she became the mother of many nations. The woman was created to support man in his endeavours and bear children to fill the earth.

In the book of Titus, the woman has another responsibility, which is to love her husband and her children, to be sensible, to think right, to be pure, chaste, virtuous, and sexually faithful to her husband in every way. The woman also is to be preoccupied with who she is, not how she looks. First Timothy 2:9-10 says a woman is to be attired modestly and discreetly, with godly fear, sobriety, and modesty, She is to be modest and discreet, demonstrating godly fear.

Another responsibility of the woman in her family is to be a worker at home. Titus 2:5 describes her as a " *keeper at home.*" This doesn't simply refer to her scrubbing floors, cleaning bathrooms, and all that. It simply connotes that the home is the sphere of her labours, whatever there might be. It is not that a woman is to keep busy all the time at home, or that she can never go out to work or do other things. Neither does it mean that she's always to be doing menial tasks and home chores. What it simply means is that the home is the sphere of her divine assignment. The home is meant for keeping, and the one assigned by God to do that task is the woman. God will not do for you what you are meant to do.

The woman is to be the home keeper, she is to take care of her husband, and to provide for him and their children all that they need as they live in the home. Materially, she is to translate the resources her husband brings home into a comfortable and blessed life for her family. She is to take the spiritual things she knows and learns, and to pass them on to her children. She is a keeper at home. She must accept the responsibility to pray for the family. If she does not, no one else will.

There is no one who can pray as passionately for your family like you would. You alone know the true state of your home, so you are in the best position to know what to do to keep it safe from all forms of wickedness. That is why my husband often testifies that he has not had the first concern over our home, because I have consistently stood in my place as a keeper of the home. I have always taken what my husband provides, including the vision of the ministry God has committed into his hands, and passed them unto the children and every other member of our household.

No concern has ever risen, because everyone knows where to fit in per time. That shall also become your testimony, in Jesus name.

Duties of the Children

The injunction to dwell according to knowledge was specifically addressed to the men. However, children also need to know their responsibilities to their parents, in order to enjoy family success. Ephesians 6:1-3 clearly states:

> *"Children, obey your parents in the Lord: for this is right.*
>
> *Honour thy father and mother; which is the first commandment with promise;*
>
> *That it may be well with thee, and thou mayest live long on the earth."*

Honour for your parents is a commandment. In fact, this scripture says it is the first commandment with a promise attached to it. The reason we find a lot of people today who can't seem to make it in life, inspite of their hard work, is perhaps because they have dishonoured their parents. If you want to see good, then obedience to God's command is required. Showing honour and respect to your parents is a commandment that is not negotiable. It does not have any given conditions when it may be disobeyed. That means whether your parents are good or bad, insensitive or irrational, born again or not, no matter their state, honour for them is a must.

The American Heritage Dictionary defines "honour" as "esteem due or paid to worth; high estimation; respect; consideration; reverence; veneration; manifestation of respect or reverence." That means you are to give to your parents due respect and reverence, and esteem them highly under every circumstances of life.

For failure to honour his father, Reuben lost his glorious place in destiny. The Bible records in Genesis 35:22:

> *"And it came to pass, when Israel dwelt in that land, that Reuben went and lay with Bilhah his father's concubine: and Israel heard it..."*

In Genesis 49:3-4, when Jacob was pronouncing blessings on his sons, what Reuben got was this:

> *"Reuben, thou art my firstborn, my might, and the beginning of my strength, the excellency of dignity, and the excellency of power:*
>
> *Unstable as water, thou shalt not excel; because thou wentest up to thy father's bed; then defiledst thou it: he went up to my couch."*

It is sad, because Reuben by destiny was the excellency of dignity. He was by destiny supposed to be a man of dignity. But he lost it for one singular act of dishonour and lack of respect for his father.

Jesus further emphasized this point in Matthew 19:16-19:

> *"And, behold, one came and said unto him, Good Master, what good thing shall I do, that I may have eternal life? And he said unto him ... but if thou wilt enter into life, keep the commandments. He saith unto him, Which? Jesus said ... Honour thy father and thy mother..."*

Longevity on earth and eternity with God are both tied to the honour given by children to their parents. This also is part of the Ten Commandments given to Moses in Exodus 20:12. The Bible says in Ecclesiastes 4:12, *"... A threefold cord is not quickly broken."*

If you want to see many good and fulfilling days on the earth, then as a child in a family, respect for your parents is non-negotiable. You will make it, in Jesus' name!

9

Filling The Cracks

When there are cracks in the walls of a house, lizards hide there comfortably. Marriage, as I have said in the course of this book, is like a house; and the lizards of life can be likened to the devil and his agents. Any crack you allow is an open invitation to the devil to have access to your home.

"Neither give place to the devil."

Ephesians 4:27

We have earlier established the fact that commitment is fundamental to success in family life. Where there is no commitment there will be no trust, and distrust leads to cracks in the marriage. Cracks left unfilled become gullies, and with the effect of erosion, gullies become canyons! In other words, any crack you leave unattended to will, with time, deteriorate until divorce becomes inevitable.

171

Watch that Unforgiveness!

Unforgiveness is one major crack in the wall of many families today. It causes couples to hold on to issues, offences, misunderstandings and various hurts of the past, and before long there is a rift so wide that tears the family apart.

I liken unforgiveness in families to cancer. I call it family cancer. Just as cancer eats up the body, many families have been eaten up and torn apart by unforgiveness.

"Looking diligently lest any man fail of the grace of God; lest any root of bitterness springing up trouble you, and thereby many be defiled".

Hebrews 12:15

Don't give room to bitterness and unforgiveness. Learn to instantly forgive each other. In fact, you can go a step further by learning to forgive even before offences are committed. One interesting thing about anger and bitterness is that it is you who suffer its consequences, not the person you are angry with.

In fact, it is a medical fact that when you are angry, bitter or live in unforgiveness your body system is set at an imbalance, which ultimately destroys your health. A researcher is quoted as saying that one minute of depression suppresses your immune system by six hours, whereas one minute of laughter boosts your immune system by twenty-four hours. So, take heed to God's word and learn to destroy every root of bitterness and offence before it gets a chance to destroy you.

Taking Forgiveness Too Far

Let me state here that when we are talking about forgiveness, wisdom demands that you don't endanger your life in the name of forgiveness.

In cases where the man has been abusive and the woman is being threatened with death, and he has in fact actually made attempts at ending her life, she must apply wisdom here. If you are in such a situation, flee for your life!

But where your life is not endangered, though it is an abusive relationship, seek counsel from born-again, Spirit-filled marriage counsellors. You will be preserved in Jesus' name!

Formalize Your Relationship

Another crack that could affect the success of your family is that of an illegal union. Some couples have been living together for years and have even had children together without a proper marriage: no dowry has been paid, nor have they had any form of formal engagement.

The account of the first marriage recorded in Genesis 2 clearly shows us that a form of formal wedding was conducted in the Garden of Eden. Adam did not just rise up to find Eve wandering about in another part of the garden, take her home, and they two started living together. The Bible records in verse 22 that God *"...brought her unto the man."* God had to physically deliver her to Adam.

Marriage is the basis for the family. If you must enjoy a successful family, then you must first be married. Pay the dowry, if it has not been paid. The payment of some form of dowry is scriptural. That you are a Christian does not override the payment of that which is due to the parents. The Bible records in Mark 12:17:

> **"And Jesus answering said unto them, Render to Caesar the things that are Caesar's, and to God the things that are God's."**

Dowry payment is the right of the bride's family, so ensure you give it to them.

The book of Genesis records a very graphic picture of a typical wedding, and all that is required to be done. Abraham sent his servant to get a wife for his son, Isaac, from among his brethren. God prospered the servant's journey and he found Rebekah. The Bible has this recorded in Genesis 24:51-53:

> **"Behold, Rebekah is before thee, take her, and go, and let her be thy master's son's wife, as the LORD hath spoken.**

And it came to pass, that, when Abraham's servant heard their words, he worshipped the LORD, bowing himself to the earth.

And the servant brought forth jewels of silver, and jewels of gold, and raiment, and gave them to Rebekah: he gave also to her brother and to her mother precious things."

Notice that precious things were given to Laban, who was at this point acting as the head of the family, and to Rebekah's mother also.

However, I must mention that in the payment of dowry, you should watch the kind of things you present as dowry. Anything you know will affect your Christian testimony should never be given. I remember what happened when my husband and I were to get married. My parents gave my husband a list of items to bring as dowry, and the list contained some items that would affect our Christian testimony. My husband simply discussed with them how such an act could affect us in future, in the light of the Word of God, and those items were taken off the list. No parent wants to jeopardize the future of their daughter. All it takes is a right word spoken in season. The Bible says, *"How forcible are right words!"* (Job 6:25).

If you approach your parents with the right words, I am definitely sure they will listen to you. Just ask for the help of the Holy Spirit to speak as you ought to, and to make you sensitive to right timing. That way, you will win them over on your side.

Having performed all that is required, you must also ensure you obtain parental blessings. There is something about the blessings your parents pronounce on you that sticks to you until all their good wishes be established in your life. Abraham's servant did not just grab Rebekah and disappeared with her. The Bible records in Genesis 24:58-60:

> *"And they called Rebekah, and said unto her, Wilt thou go with this man? And she said, I will go.*
>
> *And they sent away Rebekah their sister, and her nurse, and Abraham's servant, and his men.*
>
> *And they blessed Rebekah, and said unto her, Thou art our sister, be thou the mother of thousands of millions, and let thy seed possess the gate of those which hate them."*

These blessings became a practical reality in her life, and indeed we are all part of the thousands of millions prophesied upon Rebekah (Gal. 4:28). You shall also experience this dimension of blessings, in Jesus' name.

Another very important aspect of formalizing your marriage is to acknowledge the place of a holy Christian wedding. In Genesis 2:22 we see God's practical involvement in the institution of marriage. He it was who gave Eve out to Adam. The Bible says:

> *"And the rib, which the LORD God had taken from man, made he a woman, and brought her unto the man."*

It will therefore, be unsafe to imagine you can survive the wickedness and attacks of the devil on the marriage institution without God. The Bible says in the last days, the devil will do more wickedly (Rev. 12:12; 2 Tim. 3:1), and since he recognizes that the peace of the earth is dependent on the family, he is attacking the family institution with all vehemence. This accounts for the alarming rate of family breakdowns today.

God is your Father, and only a bastard would desire to go outside his father's house to get married. The presence of God makes all the difference in life. What happens at Christian weddings is that God is invited to be a part of the union, occupying His primary place in your union. That cannot be overlooked. So, ensure you formalize your marriage with a proper Christian wedding. In case you are already living together or you were never married in the church, it is important that you get your pastor to arrange to bless your union, even if you cannot have an open church wedding like it is done with new couples.

It is also important to have a proper legal documentation

of your union. In God's dealing with man, He always ensures there is a token, which acts as a constant reminder of the terms of the covenant. With Noah in Genesis 8:20-22 and 9:14-17 it is the rainbow. Abraham had to undergo circumcision in Genesis 17:9-11. Even Jesus had the seal of His blood as proof of the covenant of our salvation (Heb. 8:6).

A legal backup for your marriage is not a safety device, as the world would consider it. It is simply a point of contact to remind God that you have fulfilled all righteousness concerning your marriage, and, therefore, the enemy must have no access into your family.

Formalizing your union with your spouse can help eliminate several in-roads through which the devil would have penetrated your family. So many work so hard and yet have very little or nothing to show for it, because there is a leakage in their home. Some even suffer great health challenges, because the devil has found a point of justification against them. The Bible says: *"He that diggeth a pit shall fall into it; and whoso breaketh an hedge, a serpent shall bite him" (Eccl. 10:8).*

Remember the example of Job. The devil could only reach him through the leakage of fear he opened up. He was constantly scared of the possible consequences of his children's misdemeanours, that he kept offering sacrifices to avert God's curse (Job 1:5). So, when calamity befell him he said:

"For the thing which I greatly feared is come upon me,
and that which I was afraid of is come unto me."

(Job 3:25).

Sometime ago, I shared this truth at one of our women conventions. A couple who had been living together for almost ten years without being married, and have had three children, because the lady's parents refused to consent to their marriage, decided to make peace and do the right thing. They had over the years been victims of great financial ups and downs. They invest so much and yet have very little in return. They were very zealous for the things of God; covenant practitioners, and yet victims of hell. They met the lady's family, paid the dowry, went to church and had their union blessed by one of the pastors.

Soon after, great business doors opened for them. Their lives took a new turn. They began to enjoy all manner of favours: they built their own house, and even bought a Mercedes Benz car, all through the simple act of formalizing their union! Your own testimony will be the next!

Children born in such an unholy union are also victims of life. The Bible records that the iniquities of the parents affect their children, even to the third and fourth generation (Deut. 5:9).

What is more, children raised in such unions will

likely end up in similar unions as well. If you lack respect and regards for the marriage institution, your children also will bring you great heartaches by their disregard and disrespect for it. But like that couple, take a step today to fill up this covenant crack in your union.

10

Get Started!

Family success is a reality, and much more, it is a possibility for you! You may have come to a point in your relationship where you think all hope is lost. But far from it! God can give you the second chance you desire; He is the God of a second chance.

Looking at scriptures, it is possible to think that the family unit has no chance of survival, especially if you consider the story of Adam and Eve. But you discover in the New Testament that God has not given up on the family. I believe that was why the very first miracle Jesus performed during His earthly ministry, was not to open blind eyes or heal the sick, but to take away reproach and to bring restoration to the family (Jn. 2:1-11).

By turning water into wine, Jesus demonstrated that He is interested in turning tasteless marriages or families into sweet ones; ordinary homes into miraculous ones; and colourless families into colourful ones.

But you must take the first step. You must do what that bridegroom did: invite Jesus into your union. Make Him the Governor of the feast! A long time ago, a popular plaque appeared in most homes in Nigeria, it read: "Christ is the Head of this home; the silent Listener to every conversation; the unseen Guest at every meal."

These words reveal the source of failure for many families. Christ remained the silent Listener and unseen Guest. He is never given a say in the affairs of their homes, neither is His presence acknowledged. He is treated as an unwanted guest, and no one likes to stick around in a place where they are not wanted. God will never impose Himself on any one. He said:

> *"Behold, I stand at the door, and knock: if any man hear my voice, and open the door, I will come in to him, and will sup with him, and he with me"*
>
> Revelation 3:20

He stands at the door. He does not let Himself in even though, *"with God nothing shall be impossible"* (Lk.1:37). He always waits to be invited in.

The starting point for success in your family is inviting Jesus into your home. To enjoy His presence in your family, you must ask for it because it is only those that ask that are entitled to receive (Matt. 7:7). I urge you to make Jesus Lord of your home, and He will manifest His glory there.

This invitation begins with a simple prayer said with faith in your heart. If you would like to do that, please pray this prayer out loud:

"Dear Lord Jesus Christ, I proclaim You today as my Lord and my Saviour. Forgive me my sins; wash me with Your blood. I believe You died for me, and on the third day, You rose again, that I might be justified. Right now, I believe I am forgiven, I am justified, I am saved, I am born again, I am a child of God. Thank You Lord, for saving me. Amen!"

Congratulations! You are now born again and have become a child of God, with all the attendant blessings the Bible talks about. Read this testimony, and then pray this next prayer with me, as you invite Him to become the Lord of your home.

"Somebody had offended me and I had in turn vowed never to forgive him. But as I attended the Convention and heard the devastating effect unforgiveness could have in my life, I repented of it and willingly let him (who had hurt me go). Mysteriously, a disease I had carried about in my body for some years disappeared, and I was totally healed."

- F. Eliezer

"Dear Lord Jesus Christ, having proclaimed You as my Lord and my Saviour, I now invite You to be the Lord of my family. I invite You to take absolute charge

over the affairs of this family, and I give You praise for Your continuous presence in this home. Thank You Lord, Amen."

I see miracles emerging in your home from right now, in Jesus name! Every hedge that had been broken down is restored right now!

Family success is your portion! In whatever area you have wept and sorrowed in your family, I see God turn your mourning into dancing again! No matter what you are going through in your family right now, God is stepping in, and He will turn your captivity!

Another thing to get started with, is obedience to every instruction you have received in the course of reading this book. Until knowledge graduates into action, it is mere information. The knowledge of scriptures is mere information; it is the practice of it that delivers its benefits to you. Knowledge should provoke understanding, and understanding action. God's word in James 1:22-25 says:

> *"But be ye doers of the word, and not hearers only, deceiving your own selves.*
>
> *For if any be a hearer of the word, and not a doer, he is like unto a man beholding his natural face in a glass:*
>
> *For he beholdeth himself, and goeth his way, and straightway forgetteth what manner of man he was.*

But whoso looketh into the perfect law of liberty, and continueth therein, he being not a forgetful hearer, but a doer of the work, this man shall be blessed in his deed."

Until you take steps in the light of God's word, you are only deceiving yourself. The Word works only for practitioners. For your obedience to produce rewards, it must be willing and excited obedience. Willingness is a condition God has set for anything that will produce results. God's word says in Isaiah 1:19, *"If ye be willing and obedient, ye shall eat the good of the land."*

There is good in your marriage, but it will take willing obedience to eat it. Any step you take in obedience to God's word will always guarantee a reward.

One Sister Sarah T. shared this very amazing testimony, to show that obedience to God's word has rewards. Her husband, who was not born again, tested positive to HIV. Consistently, the man would challenge her faith, as he demanded submission to him in her marital responsibilities. Each time she succumbed to him, she would remind the Lord that she was acting in obedience to His word on submission. The man eventually died of AIDS. To the glory of God, this sister went for test and was found to be HIV negative.

When you step out in faith and choose to obey God,

inspite of all odds, God will always rise up to defend you. So, don't be afraid to take any step in line with what you have learnt in this book. God is determined to back you up and give you a bright testimony.

This is your day for family success. Be blessed!

ABOUT THE AUTHOR

FAITH ABIOLA OYEDEPO has brought hope, joy and life into many homes in her generation.

Having received a ministry for building godly homes, she has dedicated her life to showing people God's perfect will for their homes, and helping to lead them back there. Her weekly newspaper column, Family Matters, has helped, in no small way, in achieving this goal.

She has shown in practical terms, and through deep spiritual insight that the home can be the Eden God created it to be.

Pastor Faith has written more than 10 books, including: Marriage Covenant, Making Marriage Work and Raising Godly Children.

An anointed preacher of the gospel, Pastor Faith Oyedepo has been doggedly supportive of her husband (Bishop David Oyedepo) in the undaunting work of the ministry. She has four children — David Jnr., Isaac, Love and Joys.

Other Books by Faith A. Oyedepo

Making Marriage Work

Marriage Covenant

Raising Godly Children

You Can Overcome Anxiety

The Dignity Of The Believer

A Living Witness

Communion Table

Nurturing The Incorruptible Seed

Service: The Master Key

Stirring Up The Grace Of God

Building A Successful Family

The Spirit of Faith

Visit our website for weekly articles
by the author:

http://www.davidoyedepoministries.org